Striking the Root

Lawrence W. Reed

To Joe Fitzsimmons!

Larry Reed
2/12/08

Dedicated to the Memory of

Joseph P. Overton

1960-2003

CONTENTS

PREFACE

This humble collection of essays is offered in memory of my best friend and most valued professional colleague, Joe Overton. Nearly five years after his tragic and sudden passing, I still think of him every day.

An essay on Page 51 will tell the reader more about him. Joe would probably be embarrassed by my praise in that column; he was modest, unpretentious, often reticent. When he wasn't saying great things, he was reading, thinking or doing them. A favorite quote of his, from philosopher Henry David Thoreau, was the inspiration for my title: "There are a thousand hacking at the branches of evil to one who is striking at the root."

All of the 24 essays herein have been published before, most of them in my "Ideas and Consequences" column in The Freeman, the magazine of the Foundation for Economic Education (www.fee.org).* They do not bolster some profound, central thesis, but they do share a common thread: The superiority of individual liberty over all forms of political coercion. The essays are grouped in three sections, based on the quotes that follow this preface: "A Definition of Terms," which explores various misconceptions that undermine our freedom; "A Necessary Spring," which reflects on the essential virtues of a free people; and "The Triumphant Future," which discusses signs we'll see on the road to our inevitable destiny of freedom.

I've selected these essays because each attempts to strike at the root of coercion. I hope this small addition to the vast literature of liberty will win a convert or two.

I wish to thank the following people for their assistance: Justin Marshall, director of advancement at the Mackinac Center for Public Policy, for his early help in reconciling published versions with my previous drafts; Benjamin Stafford, a senior this year at Hillsdale College, for his editing assistance; Sheldon Richman, editor of The Freeman, for his permission to reprint the essays that appeared originally in my regular column; Thomas Shull, the Mackinac Center's senior editor, for his suggestions about the organization of this book; Ted O'Neil for first-rate editing; and Daniel Montgomery, for the design and graphics that grace this volume.

Finally, I owe a very special thanks to my dear friends Ethelmae Humphreys, Sally von Behren and James Rodney for their support of, and endless patience with, the preparation of this volume.

Lawrence W. Reed
November 2007

---

* The columns republished here have been lightly edited for currency, clarity and style.

"The beginning of wisdom is the definition of terms."

— *A saying attributed to the ancient Greeks*

"It is substantially true that virtue or morality is a necessary spring of popular government. The rule, indeed, extends with more or less force to every species of free government."

— *George Washington, presidential farewell address, 1796*

You cannot fight against the future. Time is on our side.

— *William Ewart Gladstone, 1866*

A Definition of Terms

Freedom or Free-for-All?

Imagine playing a game — baseball, cards, Monopoly or whatever — in which there was only one rule: *anything goes.*

You could discard the instruction book from the start and make things up as you go. If it "works," do it. If it "feels good," why not? If opposing players have a disagreement (an obvious inevitability) — well, you can just figure that out later.

What kind of a game would this be? Chaotic, frustrating, unpredictable, impossible. Sooner or later, the whole thing would degenerate into a mad free-for-all. Somebody would have to knock heads together and bring order to the mess.

Simple games would be intolerable played this way, but for many deadly serious things humans engage in — from driving on the highways to waging war — the consequences of throwing away the instruction book can be almost too frightful to imagine.

The business of government is one of those deadly serious things, and like a game run amok, it's showing signs that the players don't care much for the rules any more, if they even know them at all.

Don't think for a moment that by use of the term "players" I'm pointing fingers at politicians and somehow absolving everyone else of responsibility. In a sense, all of us are players; it's just that some are more actively so than others, and of those who are active, some are more destructively so than the rest. At the very least, every citizen has a stake in the outcome.

The most profound political and philosophical trend of our time is a serious erosion of any consensus about what government is supposed to do and what it's *not* supposed to do. The "instruction books" on this matter are America's founding documents, namely the Declaration of Independence and the original Constitution with its Bill of Rights. In the spirit of those great works, most Americans once shared a common view of the proper role of government: the protection of life and property.

Jefferson himself phrased it with typical eloquence: "Still one thing more fellow citizens — a wise and frugal government, which shall restrain men from injuring one another, shall leave them otherwise free to regulate their own pursuits of industry and improvement, and shall not take from the mouth of labor the bread it has earned. This is the sum of good government."

Today, there is no common view of the proper role of government or, if there is one, it is light-years from Jefferson's. Far too many people think that government exists to do anything for anybody any time they ask for it, from day care for their children to handouts for artists.

In a series of lectures to senior high school classes once, I asked the students what they thought the responsibilities of government were. I heard "Provide jobs" far more often than I heard anything like "Guarantee our freedoms." (In fact, I think the only time I heard the latter was when I said it myself.)

An organization called the Communitarian Network made news recently when it called for government to make organ donations mandatory, so that each citizen's body after death could be "harvested" for the benefit of sick people. A good cause, for sure, but is it really a duty of government to take your kidneys?

Americans once understood and appreciated the concept of individual rights and entertained very little of this nonsense. But there is no consensus today even on what a right *is,* let alone which ones we as free citizens should be free to exercise.

When the Reagan administration proposed abolishing subsidies to Amtrak, the nationalized passenger rail service, I was struck by a dissenter who phrased her objection on national television this way: "I don't know how those people in Washington expect us to get around out here. We have a right to this service."

When Congress voted to stop funding the printing of Playboy magazine in Braille, the American Council of the Blind filed suit in federal court, charging that the congressional action constituted censorship and the denial of a basic right.

The lofty notion that individuals possess certain rights — definable, inalienable and sacred — has been cheapened and mongrelized beyond anything our Founders would recognize. When those gifted individuals asserted rights to "freedom of speech" or "freedom of the press" or "freedom of assembly," they did not mean to say that one has a right to be given a microphone, a printing press, a lecture hall or a Playboy magazine at someone else's expense.

Indeed, the Founders' concept of rights did not require the initiation of force against others, or the elevation of any "want" to a lawful lien on the life or property of any other citizen. Each individual was deemed a unique and sovereign being, requiring only that others deal with him either voluntarily or not at all. It was this notion of rights that became an important theme of America's founding documents. It is the *only* notion of rights that does not yield a strife-ridden mob in which every person has his hands in every other person's pockets.

Millions of Americans today believe that as long as the cause is "good," it's a duty of government. They look upon government as a fountain of happiness and material goods. Our Founders wrote a Constitution that contains a Bill of Rights, separation of powers, checks and balances, and dozens of "thou shalt nots" directed at government itself. They knew, unlike many Americans today, that a government without rules or boundaries that does anything for anybody and confuses rights with wants will lead to intolerable tyranny.

We have tossed away the instruction book and until we find it and give it life and meaning in our public lives, we will drift from one intractable crisis to the next. Something more important than any handout from the state — namely, our liberty — hangs in the balance.

April 1994

GOVERNMENT EDUCATION REINVENTS GOVERNMENT

Perhaps the most important principle one can ever learn about the nature of government is this: It is different from all other institutions in society because it is the only one that can legally initiate force. Unfortunately, it is a principle that has been largely erased from the American memory bank. More than a hundred years of compulsory public education may be largely to blame.

Let's get something straight before we go any further. To note that government rests on the use of force is not some radical, anarchist idea. It is the very definition of the institution and its ultimate distinguishing feature. For much of the last half millennium, political scientists of virtually every stripe accepted the notion as fact. No respectable scholar tried to paper it over and pass government off as some kind of voluntary, benevolent society.

America's Founders understood this principle well and crafted a regime that never purported to eliminate force; they sought only to restrict it to a narrow sphere of life and thereby preserve a large measure of individual liberty. George Washington reportedly observed, "Government is not reason. It is not eloquence — it is force! Like fire it is a dangerous servant and a fearful master."* In other words, even when government does no more than what he wanted it to do, and when it does those few things very well as a "servant" of the people, it's still dangerous, because behind it all is the employment of legalized force.

---

* Since the original publication of this essay, I have learned from the Library of Congress that this quote, which is widely and regularly attributed to George Washington, does not appear in his writings, reducing the likelihood he actually said it. Nevertheless, the general sentiment is one Washington shared. He was persuaded, for instance, to fight for independence from Great Britain by Thomas Paine's "Common Sense," whose first chapter opens with this famous passage:

> SOME writers have so confounded society with government, as to leave little or no distinction between them; whereas they are not only different, but have different origins. Society is produced by our wants, and government by our wickedness; the former promotes our happiness positively by uniting our affections, the latter negatively by restraining our vices. The one encourages intercourse, the other creates distinctions. The first is a patron, the last a punisher.

> Society in every state is a blessing, but government even in its best state is but a necessary evil; in its worst state an intolerable one; for when we suffer, or are exposed to the same miseries by a government, which we might expect in a country without government, our calamities is [*sic*] heightened by reflecting that we furnish the means by which we suffer! Government, like dress, is the badge of lost innocence; the palaces of kings are built on the ruins of the bowers of paradise.

A deeply rooted understanding of this inherent character of government is a pillar of the free society. It's the yellow caution light that prompts wise and peaceful citizens to deliberate long and hard before accepting an expansion of government duties. It creates a healthy skepticism about seductive schemes to supplant private initiative with public action. It discourages attempts to impose a collective conformity at the expense of the individual.

If you are an advocate of the free society today, you surely have noticed erosion in the understanding of this principle. It may not be an exaggeration to assert that the erosion has been massive and far more deleterious to our liberty and well-being than all but a few ever imagined.

This point struck me hard recently when I read a letter to the editor of a local newspaper. The letter writer was responding to a previously published commentary by a man who had argued that Ernest Hemingway opposed government funding of the arts because he felt that artists should be independent of political influence. She took issue with the commentator on the grounds that Hemingway "did accept money from benefactors." Accepting money freely given by patrons, in the mind of the letter writer, was indistinguishable from accepting money from the government.

Similarly, I have witnessed countless occasions when individuals argued that if government does something and is well intentioned, it couldn't possibly be coercive; or, that if it's "democratic," it's somehow voluntary. The mere fact that politicians are elected validates almost whatever they do as nothing more than consensual acts between altruistic adults. A much more sober and rational view of the limitations of a democratic republic, preferable though it is to any other form of government, is the one that describes it as two wolves and a lamb voting on what to have for lunch.

So it is that we've arrived at the point described by Edgar Friedenberg's 1964 classic, "Coming of Age in America," where, "American high school students viewed the government as a benign institution that one should obey because it was working for the benefit of all the people." How is it possible for such a sad state of intellectual affairs to befall a nation founded on liberty and a realistic view of the state? How did it come to be that millions of Americans recoil at the "radical" suggestion that government and legalized force are one and the same?

I can think of no other source of the problem than a century of government ("public") education. When nearly 90 percent of Americans are schooled for 12 formative years by government employees, most of whom earned their teaching degrees at government universities, why should we expect anything other than an obsequious citizenry that views government as the benevolent vicar of what Rousseau called "the general will?"

The history of American public education is replete with statements by professional government school advocates that reek of statism. Judge Archibald Douglas Murphey, founder of the public school system in North Carolina, said that government must educate because "parents know not how to instruct them. ... The state, in the warmth of her affection and solicitude for their welfare must take charge of those children and place them in school where their minds can be enlightened."

A 1914 bulletin of the U.S. Bureau of Education stated, "The public schools exist primarily for the benefit of the State rather than for the benefit of the individual." And Edward Ross, a prominent sociologist, offered the most chilling description of the role of government in education: "To collect little plastic lumps of human dough from private households and shape them on the social kneading-board."

This outcome was predictable from the earliest days of American public education, and it's no different from anything else the government comes to dominate. He who pays the piper calls the tune. It just isn't in the interests of the government or those who depend on it to sully their own nests with an honest admission that their handiwork is financed and imposed at gunpoint. As education scholar Joel Spring put it 20 years ago, "A teacher, school administrator, or elected official in charge of schools may believe that his personal values represent the general values of the community; worse, he may think that his values should be adopted by the community."

Such explicit statements notwithstanding, it would be hard and perhaps politically counterproductive to argue that today's deficient government school system derives from some grand conspiracy. To explain the appalling ignorance of the American citizenry regarding the essential nature of government, conspiracy theories are not necessary. It's sufficient simply to observe that few employees of the system will rise above immediate self-interest to even recognize, let alone propagate, the notion that government in general and their jobs in particular rest on legalized force.

What difference does all this make? A lot. I can think of no situation more hostile to liberty than a failure of a free people to tell the difference between government and everything else.

December 1999

GET RID OF THE LABELS

At least when it comes to political matters, Americans are hung up on labels. Everywhere you turn, somebody is calling somebody else some name — shorthand for what the other person's political philosophy or ideological leanings are perceived to be.

If labels inform, then they can be useful. But when they confuse or distort, they're worse than useless. Amid the general dumbing down of educational standards in recent years and the resulting degeneration of public debate, I confess to a disillusionment with the commonly used political labels. Most have become excuses for people to stop thinking.

Consider the tired, old dichotomy of "liberal" on the one hand versus "conservative" on the other. "Liberal" was once an honorable word to describe those who put liberty first. During the 20th century in America, it flip-flopped into a term for those who would gladly trade liberty for a mess of pottage from the state. Even that meaning rarely applies to any one person's view on every issue.

"Conservative" is sometimes used to describe one who wants to preserve the status quo, and at other times to describe one who wants to restore a limited role for government (at least in most economic matters), which today is hardly the status quo. The confusion only worsens when the labelers go to work on foreigners. When Mikhail Gorbachev was introducing reforms in the old Soviet Union, the American media called him a "liberal" and his old-line Stalinist opponents "conservative." American conservatives rightly wondered why their label was always attached to figures the mainstream media could easily demonize, whether foreign communists or homegrown, budget-cutting libertarians.

Quite often somebody attaches an adjective to an already-confusing label that rarely clarifies anything. Take "compassionate" conservative, for example. I know a lot of very generous, caring, self-described conservatives who routinely give far more of their own resources to worthy causes than the most sanctimonious, guilt-ridden "liberals." These "conservatives" wonder why any adjective is necessary.

And how about that word "moderate?" That's been sanctified to describe one who occupies a lofty perch of enlightened and thoughtful objectivity. Look closer and you usually find a person who hasn't done his homework and can't make his mind up. And when he finally does come to a conclusion, it's strikingly inconsistent with other half-baked views he holds.

Maybe we need a new set of labels. Or perhaps we need to recognize that shorthand just won't do the job when talking about how complex principles apply to current-day issues.

In any event, if we must label people this or that, I suggest we do so in more meaningful ways, with fewer sound bites and single-word monikers. That suggests we not use one-size-fits-all descriptions, but rather that we describe traits and tendencies.

For starters: Why not differentiate between those who are satisfied with rhetoric versus those who demand results?

People who advocate government-financed and government-directed efforts to address problems once widely regarded as personal, private or "civil society" responsibilities almost always settle for rhetoric alone. Perhaps that's because their handiwork rarely produces results worth bragging about. To these people, it is usually enough for someone to simply declare his concern for the poor to prove that he really cares. It doesn't matter that government programs to help the poor have decisively accomplished the very opposite, a painful fact that both experience and economics should have forecast in advance.

People who advocate nongovernmental solutions — changes in attitudes and behavior, strengthening the family, involvement of churches and private associations, for example — are not typically animated by rhetoric. They are focused on results, and they have the incredible story of the American experience to which they can proudly point. It wasn't rhetoric that carved a great civilization out of wilderness; it wasn't self-righteous breast-beating or mere professions of concern that fed, clothed and housed more people at higher levels than any other society ever known in history. It was a combination of strong families, rugged self-reliance, effective volunteer associations, wealth-creating private initiative and risk-taking entrepreneurship.

Here's another meaningful way to categorize people's thinking: those who are happy with short-term answers versus those who plan for the long run.

Some people think only of the here-and-now, what strikes the eye, the present moment. Others see further ahead and recognize that quick fixes often yield long-term disaster.

In this regard, those who favor government "solutions" are on the short end of the stick. The primary answer they offer to problems such as poverty is to toss the poor a government check. They observe the subject spending the check on groceries and conclude that they have done good. But those who support nongovernmental solutions know the meaning of the adage, "Give me a fish and I eat for a day; teach me to fish and I eat for a lifetime."

Yet another possible method of drawing distinctions and applying accurate descriptions: those who exhibit little interest in liberty versus those who understand that without liberty, little else either matters or is possible.

People who push government to "tax and tax, spend and spend, elect and elect" (in the words of FDR brain truster Harry Hopkins) are more than willing to sacrifice a little liberty for the sake of a handout. More appropriately, they are willing to sacrifice the liberties of everyone for the sake of handouts for a few. Those who prefer private, nongovernmental measures to address problems understand that government has nothing to give anybody except what it first takes from somebody, and that government that is big enough to give you everything you want has become big enough to take away everything you've got.

Instead of settling for today's standard and increasingly confusing or irrelevant labels, we should concentrate on explaining that the ideas worth supporting are those that are tested and found worthwhile because they produce results, not rhetoric; that the ideas worth supporting are those that do not mortgage the future for the sake of the present; and finally, that the ideas worth supporting are those that do not treat other people's liberty as though it were so much scrap paper waiting to be cleared away.

Surely, for reasons I've already made apparent, one who values freedom and free markets can readily embrace these new criteria for pegging political/economic tendencies. We'll probably have a very hard time, however, getting the other side to go along. But that fact says volumes about the merits of their positions and certainly tells us all a lot more than the old mainstream *mis*labels. If insisting on this approach compels a few to dig a little deeper and learn more than what can fit on a bumper sticker, public debate will to some degree be better-informed.

January 2001

Don't Expect Much From Politics

The older I get and the more I learn from observing politics, the more obvious it is that it's no way to run a business — or almost anything else, for that matter. The deficiencies, absurdities and perverse incentives inherent in the political process are powerful enough to frustrate anyone with the best of intentions. It frequently exalts ignorance and panders to it. And a few notable exceptions aside, it tends to attract the most mediocre talent with motives that are questionable at best.

Recently, the ninth child of Robert and Ethel Kennedy, Max Kennedy, flirted with the idea of running for political office. A story in the July 15, 2001, New York Times Magazine recounted his ill-fated attempt at a stump speech riddled with trite one-liners like these: "I want to fight for all of you. I'll commit myself heart and soul to be the kind of congressman who cares about you. I'll dedicate myself to fighting for working families to have a fair chance. I make you this one pledge: I will always be there for you."

Kennedy's handler pressed him repeatedly for a "take-away message," something of substance that his audience would remember. "What do you want people to take away from it?" he asked several different ways. The would-be candidate stammered and couldn't think of much other than "I'm a nice guy" until finally he admitted: "I don't know. Whatever it has to be."

Eligible for public office? Certainly, though in this case the subject fizzled out before his campaign was ever lit, and he has presumably found useful work elsewhere. Hundreds just like Max Kennedy get elected every year. But would it ever occur to you to put someone who talks this way in charge of your business? Outside of politics, is there any other endeavor in which such nonsense is as epidemic?

Welcome to the silly side of politics. It's characterized by no-speak, doublespeak and stupidspeak — the use of one's tongue, lips and other speechmaking body parts to sway minds without ever educating them, and deceiving them if necessary. The serious side of politics comes afterward when the elected actually do something, even if — as is often the case — it bears little resemblance to what they promised. It's serious business in any case because it's the part where coercion puts flesh on the rhetorical bones. What makes a politician a politician, and differentiates politics from all other walks of life, is that the politician's words are backed up by his ability to employ legal force.

This is not a trivial point. After all, in the grand scheme of life there are ultimately only two ways to get what you want. You can rely on voluntary action (work, production, trade, persuasion and charity) or you can swipe. Exemplars of voluntary action are Mother Teresa, Henry Ford, Bill Gates, Stephen Spielberg and the kid who delivers your newspaper. When someone who isn't elected or appointed to any post in government swipes something, he's a thief.

If acting in his capacity as a government official, one who might otherwise be thought of as a thief is considered at least by many to be a "public servant." And he's not swiping; he's "appropriating."

Things that rely on the regular affirmation of voluntary consent don't look at all like those that rest on force. Whereas mutual consent encourages actual results and accountability, the political process puts a higher premium on the mere promise or claim of results and the shifting of blame to other parties.

To win or keep your patronage and support, a provider of goods or services must manufacture something of real value. A business that doesn't produce or a charity that doesn't meet a need will quickly disappear. To get your vote, one politician only has to look or sound better than the next, even if both of them would renege on more pledges than they would keep. In the free marketplace, you almost always get what you pay for and pay for what you get. As a potential customer, you can say, "No, thanks," and take a walk. In politics the connection between what you pay for and what you actually get is problematic at best.

This is another way of asserting that your vote in the marketplace counts for so much more than your vote in the polling booth. Cast your dollars for the washing machine of your choice and that's what you get — nothing more and nothing less. Pull the lever for the politician of your choice and most of the time, if you're lucky, you'll get some of what you do want and much of what you don't. And the votes of a special-interest lobby may ultimately cancel yours out.

Some politicians like to rail against a practice in the private sector they call "bundling." If you want to buy a company's computer operating system, for example, you may also have to buy its Internet browser. That's not much different from what happens at your local bookstore: You may want only Chapter One, but you've got to buy the whole book. But if bundling is a crime, then politics is Public Enemy No. 1. In some elections the options range from Scarface to Machine Gun Kelly. Politics may not be the oldest profession, but the results are often the same.

These important distinctions between voluntary, civil society and coercion-based government explain why in politics the Max Kennedy types are the rule rather than the exception. Say little or nothing, or say silly things, or say one thing and do another — and your prospects of success may only be enhanced. When the customers are captives, the seller may just as easily be the one who whispers seductive nonsense in their ears as the one who puts something real on their plates.

Like it or not, people judge private, voluntary activities by a higher standard than they do public acts of the political process. That's all the more reason to keep politics a small and isolated corner of our lives. We all have so many more productive things to tend to.

December 2001

To Own or Be Owned: That Is the Question

President George W. Bush's "Ownership Society" proposals didn't get very far, but for a brief moment, they stimulated national discussion in directions politicians feared to tread for decades. They also gave some of us an opportunity to remind the American public of some critically important truths.

The fact is, "ownership" as a general concept is never at issue in any society. It is neither possible nor desirable to construct a society in which people or the material things they create are not "owned." Either you will "own" yourself or someone else will own you. As far as material things are concerned, somebody must own them, too. Those "somebodies" will either be those who created them, received them as a gift or traded freely for them, or they will be those who took them by force. There is no middle ground, no "third way" in which ownership is somehow avoided.

Indeed, ownership is both a virtue and a necessity. What is yours, you tend to husband. If it belongs to someone else, you have little incentive to care for it. If it belongs to "everyone" — the nebulous, collectivist approach — then you have every incentive to use and abuse it.

Ownership is nothing less than the right to shape, use and dispose. Even if you have legal title to something, you wouldn't think you really "owned" it if the government told you what, how and when you could do anything with it; in that instance, the government would be the de facto owner. Ownership is control and the real owner of anything is the controller.

For thoroughly trashing the resources of any society, no more surefire prescription exists than to take them from those to whom they belong (the rightful owners) and give them to those who simply think they have a better idea of what to do with them. Think "Soviet."

The myth of "common ownership" only muddies the issue. Public parks are thought of as "the people's property," but that really means that the government owns them; the taxpayers pay the bill; and the public gets to use them according to the rules established and enforced by the government. The post office was once touted as an example of "common ownership," but anybody who ever showed up at the counter to demand his share was probably surprised how fast the service can be.

It's either you or somebody else. Who should own your retirement savings — you or the government? Who should own your health care dollars — you, the government or some third-party payer you'd prefer to avoid? Who should decide where your child goes to school — you the parent, or a handful of *other* parents different from you only by virtue of the fact that they work for the government?

In this light, President Bush's offerings actually appeared downright modest. Even if passed without modification, the government would still "own" a large majority share of each American's Social Security dollars. Government and third-party payers would still dominate the health care market, and most parents who want to send their children to schools other than government schools wouldn't get much of a break.

But the ferocity and the shallowness with which the ideological opposition in Congress has responded speak volumes about where their core values really are. To many, it's more important that government be in control and you be dependent upon it than that your retirement savings be secure, your health care needs be taken care of or your children be well-educated. They are the control freaks among us, and some of them will not be satisfied until they own the rest of us lock, stock and barrel.

To own or be owned. Take your pick.

February 2005

THE GOLDEN CALF OF DEMOCRACY

No one knew better how to deflate the inflated than the late political satirist and commentator H.L. Mencken. "Democracy," he once said, "is the theory that the common people know what they want, and deserve to get it good and hard." He also famously defined an election as "an advance auction of stolen goods." With so many promises made in elections to so many, his description seems especially fitting.

Mencken was not opposed to democracy. He simply possessed a more sobering view of its limitations than does today's conventional wisdom, which regards it as the unmentioned fourth branch of the Trinity.

Democracy may be the world's single most misunderstood concept of political governance. Commonly romanticized, it is assumed in most circles to ensure far more than it possibly can. The Norman Rockwell portrait of engaged, informed citizens contending freely on behalf of the common good is the utopian ideal that obscures the very messy details of reality.

Pure, undiluted democracy would be unshackled majority rule. Everybody would vote on everything, and 50 percent plus one extra vote would decide every "public" issue — and inevitably, a lot of what ought to be private ones, too. Ancient Athens for a brief time came closest to this, but no society of any size and complexity can practice this form of governance for very long. It's unwieldy, endlessly contentious and disrespectful of the inalienable rights of individuals who find themselves in the minority.

People like the sound of "democracy" because it implies that all of us have an equal say in our government, and that a simple majority is somehow inherently fair and smart in deciding issues. Subjecting every decision of governance to a vote of the people, however, is utterly impossible. Many decisions have to be made quickly and require knowledge that few people possess or have the time to become expert on. Many decisions don't belong in the hands of any government at all.

Suppose someone says, "I just don't like people with boats and jewelry. I think we should confiscate their property. Let's have a vote on that." A democratic purist would have to reply, "All in favor say 'Aye!'" Anyone interested in protecting individual rights would have to say, "That's *not* a proper function of government, and even if 99 percent of the citizens vote for it, it's still wrong."

In common parlance, "democracy" has been stretched to mean little more than responsive government. Because of such things as elections, government officials cannot behave in a vacuum. That fact is laudable, but it hardly guarantees that government will be good or limited. Even the best and most responsive of governments still rests upon the legal use of force — an inescapable fact that requires not blind and fawning reverence, but brave, intelligent and determined vigilance.

Elections are a political safety valve for dissident views, because they rely on ballots instead of bullets to resolve disputes. They allow for political change without resorting to violence to make change happen — but the change a majority favors can be right or wrong, good or evil. The folks who work to make it easier to vote so more votes are cast should also spend their time encouraging others to be well-informed before they vote.

In spite of candidates singing interminable paeans to "our democracy," America is thankfully not one and never has been. Our Founders established a republic, modifying democracy considerably. It provides a mechanism whereby almost anyone can have some say in matters of government. We can run for office. We can support candidates and causes of our choosing. We can speak out in public forums. And, indeed, some issues are actually decided by majority vote.

But a sound republic founded on principles that are more important than majority rule (like individual rights) will put strong limits on all this. In its Bill of Rights, our Constitution clearly states, "Congress shall make no law. ..." It does not say, "Congress can pass anything it wants so long as a majority supports it."

If you worship the golden calf called democracy, you might want to think about finding a different religion.

November 2004

A THINK TANK FOR THOSE WHO DON'T THINK

"The ideas of economists and political philosophers, both when they are right and when they are wrong," wrote John Maynard Keynes, "are more powerful than is commonly understood. Indeed the world is ruled by little else."

Keynes was wise to include the phrase, "both when they are right and when they are wrong." Unfortunately, it's all too true that good ideas must compete with bad ideas and sometimes, at least temporarily, the bad ones win out. Worse yet, even a silly or superstitious notion that barely rises to the level of an idea can wield great influence. And in our midst are crackpots who dredge up discredited and discarded ideas, dress them up in new disguise and hawk them all over again.

Imagine a group of people — now, not 500 years ago — who insist that the world is flat and that the sun revolves around it. They seek to propagate these concepts to a broader audience, so they form the Society of Flat Earthers. Ignoring science and experience, they turn out papers and hold meetings to contradict the conventional wisdom. We would demand proof of their claim, not mere flimsy rhetoric, as we heap on them mounds of evidence to the contrary. While we might be tempted to applaud their zeal, most men and women of sound mind would write them off as misguided, mystical or mad.

In these enlightened times a Society of Flat Earthers seems beyond the pale. But something close to it was unveiled in Washington only last summer. The subject was not the hard science of physics or astronomy but the more pliable disciplines of political science and economics.

An article in the Aug. 14, 2002, Washington Post announced that a new "socialist think tank" was being formed in Washington, D.C., called the American Socialist Foundation. Its officials declared that they would "focus on contemporary economic and political issues and develop socialist analysis and policies to address them." Among other things, their secretary-treasurer was quoted as saying, "Socialists favor public ownership of the media."

I acknowledge that I am in the think-tank business myself. A reader might easily interpret any skepticism about this group on my part as a bit of competitive pique. I want to say up front that it's not the competition that bothers me; rather, it's the preposterous assumption implicit in the very announcement of a "socialist think tank." Putting those words in juxtaposition is no different from placing "fire" aside "ice" or putting "chaste" next to "Bill Clinton." Use one or the other, but don't put them in the same phrase, please.

"Socialism" and "think tank" are, in my humble view, mutually exclusive terms. Arguably, "socialism" is the opposite of "think." It does, however, produce lots of tanks — tanks to suppress people who actually do think. The one quintessential, unassailable truth that distills from centuries of experience with socialism is that when it isn't arrogantly bossing people around, it's stifling, strangling or killing them. It is based on the ludicrous assumption that people who have a hard time planning their own lives, and often fail at it, can nonetheless plan the lives of not just a handful of others around them, but the lives of millions they don't even know! The result has been everywhere and in all times what Ludwig von Mises brilliantly described decades ago as "Planned Chaos."

State ownership of the media. Now there's a winner of an idea, or so argues the new socialist think tank. In free markets, one can not only purchase at minuscule cost an almost infinite array of viewpoints, one can also buy a printing press or a bullhorn or a company and manufacture one or more viewpoints oneself. What's the point of state ownership, financed by taxation? Only an idiot would argue that state ownership broadens and multiplies available opinion; state ownership invariably exerts a coercive bias in the public square — limiting, if not ultimately monopolizing, opinion. When socialists come to power, their attitudes and actions are never inclusive and inviting. "Why think when a tank will do?" would seem to be their guiding principle.

There are some settled truths in the world, derived from such things as science, economics, human experience, facts, evidence, reason and logic. The sun comes up in the east. The earth is spherical. Markets are immeasurably more rational and productive than central planning and state ownership. Heavens, isn't that what even a moron should sense from the failure of every short-lived socialist "paradise" the planet has ever known?

While it's tempting to cite reams of research, piles of statistics and mounds of bodies to make the case against socialism, that's been done rather thoroughly by countless others. I rest my case against it on the observation that socialism by definition does not rely on the free will and peaceful interaction of sovereign individuals to verify its efficacy. Indeed, the very fact that it reduces to force is testimony to its manifest failure. If I'm suspicious of any notion that favors the dragoons over persuasion, the fist over the podium, then I guess I'm guilty of favoring civilization over barbarism.

Socialists take aquariums and turn them into fish soup. The endless socialist quest for whatever it is socialists quest for all adds up to pitifully little — nothing more, in fact, than what French economist Frédéric Bastiat dismissed more than a century and a half ago as "legalized plunder."

So it is that this new organization in Washington, devoted to socialism, is not a think tank, or I'm Florence Nightingale. It is a Ministry of Propaganda dedicated to advancing mysticism and nonsense. Central planning, state ownership, lots of bureaucracy seizing and spending other people's money — the essence of socialism, in other words — should no longer be elevated shamelessly to the status of a respectable science.

Diversity of ideas is a great thing, a pillar of a free and enlightened society. No inane scribbling should ever be outlawed, no matter how unpopular. But that doesn't mean every inane scribbling deserves the status and esteem of an argument. Monarchy as a political concept may still have a kernel of a credible case, but socialism as an economic system does not. It's been tried a million times. It doesn't work; it steals from people; and it lays waste to both the land and the spirit. Get over it.

January 2002

The Message of the Nonvoter

After every election, our ears are afflicted with a familiar whine: "Isn't it simply awful that so few people vote. What we need are laws that make it easier to vote or laws that penalize people if they don't."

Don't get me wrong. I cherish the right to vote — so much so that I don't want it belittled by those who think that just showing up at the polls is all it takes to ensure the survival of representative government. There are some people who should vote, and then there are others — millions of them, unfortunately — who would do representative government a big favor if they didn't.

Embedded in the popular complaint about the decline of voting among the American electorate is at least one assumption that is demonstrably false: that higher voter turnout is needed to somehow "make democracy work."

In the first half-century of America's experience as a nation, voter turnout was often much lower than it is today — frequently less than 20 percent of adult males actually cast ballots. Part of this is explained by the presence of property requirements for voting in many states. Most of our Founders and early leaders believed that people ought to have a direct and personal stake in the system before they could vote on who should run it. The fact that in those years we managed with low voter turnout to elect the likes of Washington, Jefferson, Madison and Adams suggests that maybe we should make voting more difficult, not easier — a privilege to be earned, not an unbridled right to be abused.

Then there are those who want to make it so easy to vote that you wonder how anything so costless could be the least bit meaningful. Some years ago, I read a blurb about a Colorado organization called "Vote by Phone." I don't know if the group is still around, but the idea still is — allowing Americans to cast their votes on election day by telephone from home instead of at local polling stations.

Under the plan, all registered voters would be given 14-digit voter identification numbers. Voters would call a toll-free number from touch-tone phones, punch in their ID numbers and vote on candidates and ballot issues by punching other numbers.

Whether or not the science exists to resolve the inherent technical, security and privacy questions, there exists no reason at all to make voting any easier than it currently is. Low voter turnout does not endanger our political system. Here's what does: politicians who lie, steal or create rapacious bureaucracies, voters who don't know what they are doing and people who think that either freedom or representative government will be preserved by pulling levers or punching ballot cards or making phone calls.

The right to vote, frankly, is too important to be cheapened and wasted by anyone who does not understand the issues and the candidates. The uninformed would be doing their duty for representative government if they either became informed or left the decisions at the ballot box up to those who are. How did the idea that voting for the sake of voting is a virtue ever get started anyhow?

Our political system — resting as it does on the foundations of individual liberty and a republican form of government — is also endangered by people who vote for a living instead of working for one. They use the political process to get something at everyone else's expense, voting for the candidates who promise them subsidies, handouts and special privileges. This is actually anti-social behavior that erodes both our freedoms and our representative form of government by conferring ever more power and resources upon the politically well-connected and the governing elite. I don't know about you, but I don't want these people to have it so easy that all they have to do is pick up a phone to pick my pocket.

Surely, the right to vote is precious and vital enough to be worth the effort of a trip to the polling place. Anyone who won't do that much for good government isn't qualified to play the game. Moreover, politicians who bemoan ever lower voter turnout shouldn't be so critical of nonvoters. If a nonvoter's excuse is that he doesn't know what he should to vote intelligently, he should be thanked for avoiding decisions he's unprepared to make and encouraged to educate himself. If a nonvoter is simply disgusted with lies and broken promises, then maybe it's the *politicians* who should listen and learn; the nonvoters are trying to tell them something.

Sure, it would be nice if more people voted — but only if they know what they're doing and if they're not doing it to grab something that doesn't belong to them. There's nothing about voting by telephone or other such schemes that makes people smarter or more honest, and there's nothing about stuffing the ballot box with more paper that ensures either freedom or representative government.

November 2002

SAVE US FROM GREAT IDEAS

I keep a "Pet Peeve" file. Among the many items it contains are several articles about a famous Michigan project that started out as somebody's "great idea." It secured government funds and then promptly went kaput. It was called AutoWorld.

In 1984, the $70 million AutoWorld theme park opened in Flint, Mich., amid much fanfare and hoopla. Situated on nearly seven acres of land downtown, the park was supposed to draw 900,000 visitors every year and help revive a dying inner city. It had the enthusiastic support of city and state officials and many big-name Flint citizens. Half the $70 million it took to build the facility came from federal, state and city governments.

Sixteen years later, nothing remains of the park. Closed after less than two years of sparse crowds and later demolished, the site is now part of the University of Michigan's Flint campus. "Build it and they will come" turned into "Built it and they said ho-hum."

People who get "great ideas" and immediately think that government should bring them into being demean both their ideas and government. If an idea is really so great, why must force be employed? And if government is nothing more than a playground for every "great idea," then it ceases to be a protector of us all and becomes a weapon wielded by the politically well-connected at the expense of everyone else. This knee-jerk eagerness to get government involved in everything also has the effect of diminishing the important role of civil society's most civilizing institutions — the informal network of private and voluntary interactions that arise from families, friendships, churches, associations and mutually beneficial commercial transactions in a free marketplace.

Every day, somebody somewhere gets a great idea and thinks nothing of stealing from others through government to fund it. Those of us who are troubled by these trigger-happy statists need to become more active and vocal in exposing their schemes. Toward that end, I share here a story and a letter.

With echoes of the AutoWorld failure still reverberating, the city of Kalamazoo is attempting to put taxpayers on the hook for another theme park. The city-funded Kalamazoo Aviation History Museum has announced plans to build a seven-acre "Legacy of Flight" attraction — an aviation entertainment and education center slated to open in June 2003. Local leaders want the state of Michigan to come up with as much as half of the estimated $80 million construction cost. Proponents are pushing for a 25 percent hike in the local hotel accommodations tax to raise the other half. When I raised objections, its main promoter and the head of the museum, Robert Ellis, wrote me a letter in which he questioned my motives. This was my response:

Dear Mr. Ellis:

Thank you for your letter of February 28 and the invitation to visit the Aviation History Museum. When I have plans to be in the Kalamazoo area, I will give you a call.

My criticism of the Legacy of Flight museum is not of the project itself, but rather of the public funding of it through taxation. On WKZO radio a week ago, I very plainly stated that I had no doubt that the project has many interesting and informative exhibits and that if indeed it does, it ought to be able to attract plenty of paying customers to make it worthwhile. Nonetheless, since my position has prompted you to question my motives, I'd like to explain those motives to you here.

I have one motive for my position and it revolves around individual liberty and the proper role of government. If I were to concede that it is proper for government to take money from people (through taxes, which are not voluntary) for the purposes of entertaining and informing them about flight, then I suppose there is absolutely nothing that I could legitimately declare to be beyond the bounds of government. We could simply announce that government will rob Peter to pay Paul any time Paul gets a great idea.

America's Founders knew that everybody has his own ideas about what's good for others. But they also understood that just because you've got a "great idea," you don't have the right to compel other people to pay for it. The Girl Scouts have a great idea, but they sell cookies to raise money; they don't swipe it through taxes. I happen to think the Mackinac Center is doing fantastic, invaluable work but it would never occur to me to ask the politicians to tax somebody to pay for it. If state tax money goes to the Legacy of Flight, I wonder what you'd say to Grandma over in Bad Axe [Michigan], who will never visit it and has trouble paying her monthly electric bill, but who will be forced to pay for it anyway.

I am aware that people who want tax money for the Legacy of Flight project are absolutely convinced that it's different from similar government ventures in the past like AutoWorld. What else is new? That's what the AutoWorld folks said. The real test of just how different it is, however, is not rhetoric. The real test is, will people freely support it, or does it require compulsion (taxes) to make it fly?

How about if I make you a deal? I promise not to try to get politicians to take anything from you for any local projects I get excited about, if you promise not to try to get politicians to take anything from me for the projects that excite you.

American society is increasingly becoming one in which, figuratively, we are all standing in a circle with each person's hand in the next person's pocket. I think it would be courageous and principled of you if you were to declare, "I have such confidence in the Legacy of Flight project that I am going to convince people freely of its merits. I will persuade them to support it instead of taking their money through taxes whether they like it or not." You'd be a hero.

Sincerely,

Lawrence W. Reed

July 2000

Government Putts

Mark Twain once said that the game of golf was nothing more than "a good walk spoiled." But to avid golfers, such impertinence obscures a cardinal truth: The sport is infinitely complex and not for everybody.

Golf requires patience, concentration and forbearance. Distractions must be ignored or compensated for by careful advance planning. A serious player must learn from his mistakes and be earnest about continuous quality improvement. A long-term perspective is a must so that no bad day becomes a deterrent to the next match. Golf etiquette demands a healthy respect for the rights of others and a fealty to the rules. Honesty is not only the best policy in the game, it is the *only* policy for any true gentleman of golf. Percy Boomer is reputed to have said that if you want to hide your true character, don't play golf.

And while among friends one mulligan per round may be acceptable, it is unforgivable to ignore repeated failure and pass off your score as far better than it truly is.

From these unassailable facts, one certain conclusion can be derived: Golf is no legitimate concern of government. Former California Gov. George Deukmejian put it well when he observed that, "The difference between golf and government is that in golf you can't improve your lie."

Few Americans would regard golf as a core government function, but officials in one municipality apparently think it's important enough to consider swiping a private course and making it their city's very own. Earlier this year it was revealed that the Village of North Hills on New York's Long Island would like to employ eminent domain powers to condemn and seize the Deepdale Golf Club and its 18-hole course, and then convert it to city-owned links for village residents only.

Deepdale is not a cow pasture. It's one of the finest courses in the nation, a playground for the rich and famous. Comedian Bob Hope regarded it as one his favorites. North Hills is not even claiming it's "blighted" — a ploy often used by municipalities to confiscate attractive properties so they can hand them over to someone else who might pay higher taxes than the previous owners. No, the bureaucrats and political empire-builders who run North Hills just want to be in the golf business and would rather not get their hands dirty by investing their own money to build or buy one. In fact, if the seizure takes place, a private entity will go off the tax rolls and become a tax-eating public one. The compassionate, public-spirited mayor pushing the scheme says, "I only do what's in the best interests of village residents." (Muammar Ghadafi says that a lot too.)

I've always thought that if all that local governments did was keep the streets safe, the traffic moving and the sewers flowing, they would have a full-time job on their hands. I figure that if a service can be found in the Yellow Pages, it probably doesn't need to be done by the government. In my state of Michigan, we have 823 privately owned golf courses — an average of 10 for every Michigan county. But we also have 91 courses owned by various units of government, including seven owned by state universities. How do municipalities and universities find time from the conventional duties of government to manage golf courses? Could the golf distraction help explain why their conventional duties often get done poorly at excessive expense?

When a private company sells a product at a price that somebody else thinks is "below cost," you can bet that some self-anointed consumer advocate will cry "Dumping!" and demand the company raise the price. But where are the anti-dumpers when government golf courses do the same? One former private course owner in my state paid $200,000 a year in property taxes while the local municipal links paid nothing and also ran $10 specials for 18 holes. That's a big reason why the private course owner is now a *former* private course owner.

Consider the new $13.4 million county-owned Lyon Oaks Golf Course, which opened in Michigan's Oakland County in 2002. Oakland is the state's richest county, and home to no fewer than 22 of the state's 91 government-owned golf courses. Some of the taxes paid by the 70 private courses in the county go to subsidize their government competition. Furthermore, the golf expert on my staff, Michael LaFaive (he researches and writes about golf better than he plays it), determined that Lyon Oaks received three state grants worth $2.4 million and another $5.1 million from the sale of tax-exempt government bonds. Among its various, attractive amenities are a hard-to-get, state-issued liquor license. LaFaive argues that no matter how you slice it, golf courses are one big financial sand trap for taxpayers or private competitors, or both.

So does Stephen Shmanske, economist and author of the 2004 book "Golfonomics." He analyzed the record of 104 private and public golf courses in the San Francisco Bay Area between 1893 and 2001. He found that municipal links actually deterred the entry of other courses and reduced the total number in the area. Shmanske recommends privatization to increase both the number of courses and the number of golfers. That strongly counters the already weak claim that government needs to play golf so as to increase public access to the sport.

Then there's a story from the March 6, 2006, Ann Arbor News. Never mind the fact that the city's two municipal courses pay no taxes; the city has lost about another million dollars just keeping them open in spite of a 50 percent hike in fees. So far this decade, the number of rounds played has fallen by nearly half. The story says, "The city would be satisfied just to break even." City officials are having a hard time grappling with the obvious solution: Get Ann Arbor out of the golf business.

In any event, government golf makes even less sense than cents. Government shouldn't be doing pizza, bungee-jumping or dog-sitting either, and for all the same reason. These are not activities, profitable or not, that fall within the proper sphere of legal and moral coercion. It's widely accepted that government can legitimately use force (cops, courts, tanks and taxes) to keep the peace, but to whack little white balls around a field?

Gimme a break, if not a mulligan.

July 2006

An Open Letter to Statists Everywhere

Dear Statist Friends:

I know, I know. You're already objecting to my letter. You don't like the label "statist." You don't think of yourselves as worshipping government; rather, you think of yourselves as simply wanting to help people, with government being your preferred means to achieve what is usually a very worthy end. "Statist," you say, is a loaded term.

Well, let's wait and see how the term stacks up after you've read my entire letter and answered its questions. In the meantime, if you have any doubt about whether this missive is directed at you, let me clarify to whom I am writing. If you're among those many people who spend most of their time and energy advocating a litany of proposals for expanded government action, and little or no time recommending offsetting reductions in state power, then this letter has indeed found its mark.

You clever guys are always coming up with new schemes for government to do this or that, to address this issue or solve that problem, or fill some need somewhere. You get us limited-government people bogged down in the minutiae of how your proposed programs are likely to work (or not work), and while we're doing the technical homework you seldom do, you demonize us as heartless number crunchers who don't care about people.

Sometimes we all get so caught up in the particulars that we ignore the big picture. I propose that we step back for a moment. Put aside your endless list of things for government to do and focus on the whole package. I need some thoughtful answers to some questions that maybe, just maybe, you've never thought much about because you've been too wrapped up in the program du jour.

At the start of the 1900s, government at all levels in America claimed between 5 percent and 6 percent of personal income. A hundred years later, it takes around 40 percent — up by a factor of seven or more. So my first questions to you are these: Why is this not enough? How much do you want? Fifty percent? Seventy percent? Do you want all of it? To what extent do you believe a person is entitled to what he (or she) has earned?

I want specifics. Like millions of Americans planning for their retirement or their children's college education, I need to know. I've already sacrificed a lot of plans to pay your bills, but if you're aiming for more, I'm going to have to significantly curtail my charitable giving, my discretionary spending, my saving for a rainy day, my future vacations and perhaps some other worthwhile things.

I know what you're thinking: "There you go again, you selfish character. We're concerned about all the people's needs and you're only interested in your own bank account." But who is really focused on dollars and cents here, you or me?

Why is it that if I disagree with your means, you almost always assume I oppose your ends? I want people to eat well, live long and healthy lives, get the prescription drugs and health care they need, etc., etc., just like you. But I happen to think there are more creative and voluntary ways to get the job done than robbing Peter to pay Paul through the force of government. Why don't you show some confidence in your fellow citizens and assume that they can solve problems without you?

We're not ignorant and helpless, in spite of your many poorly performing government schools and our having to scrape by with a little more than half of what we earn. In fact, give us credit for managing to do some pretty amazing things even *after* you take your 40 percent cut — things like feeding and clothing and housing more people at higher levels than any socialized society has ever even dreamed of.

This raises a whole series of related questions about how you see the nature of government and what you've learned, if anything, from our collective experiences with it. I see the ideal government as America's Founders did — a "dangerous servant" employing legalized force for the purpose of preserving individual liberties. As such, it is charged with deterring violence and fraud and keeping itself small, limited and efficient. How can you profess allegiance to peace and nonviolence and at the same time call for so much forcible redistribution?

Don't invoke democracy, unless you're prepared to explain why might — in the form of superior numbers — makes right. Of course, I want the governed to have a big say in whatever government we have, but unlike you I have no illusions about any act being a legitimate function of government if its political supporters are blessed by 50 percent plus one of those who bother to show up at the polls. Give me something deeper than that, or I'll round up a majority posse to come and rightfully claim whatever we want of yours.

Why is it that you statists never seem to learn anything about government? You see almost any shortcoming in the marketplace as a reason for government to get bigger, but you rarely see any shortcoming in government as a reason for it to get smaller. In fact, I wonder at times if you are honestly capable of identifying shortcomings of government at all! Do we really have to give you an encyclopedia of broken promises, failed programs and wasted billions to get your attention? Do we have to recite all the workers' paradises that never materialized, the flashy programs that fizzled, the problems government was supposed to solve but only managed into expensive perpetuity?

Where, by the way, do you think wealth comes from in the first place? I know you're fond of collecting it and laundering it through bureaucracies — "feeding the sparrows through the horses" as my grandfather once put it — but tell me honestly how you think it initially comes into being. Come on, now. You can say it: *private initiative.*

I've asked a lot of questions here, I know. But you have to understand that you're asking an awful lot more in blood, sweat, tears and treasure from the rest of us every time you pile on more government without lightening any of the previous load. If anything I've asked prompts you to rethink your premises and place some new restraints on the reach of the state, then maybe the statist label doesn't apply to you. In which case, you can look forward to devoting more of your energies to actually solving problems instead of just talking about them, and to liberating people instead of enslaving them.

Sincerely,

Lawrence W. Reed

December 2000

AMERICA'S ECONOMICS KNOWLEDGE DEFICIT

Economics is a subject that dominates public life and important policy discussions these days, but most Americans who rely on what they've learned of it in the public schools are entering the intellectual battle unarmed.

According to an informal survey in my state of Michigan, 72 percent of the state's high schools offer economics. But of those, 51 percent make it a required course, while 49 percent offer it as an elective. Only a tiny fraction of students choose to take the subject when the choice is up to them. Barely 49 percent of Michigan students had actually completed one economics course before graduation in 1992.

The survey involved no value judgments regarding the kind of economics taught. Some courses deal with little more than consumer issues: how to balance a checkbook, how to find the best deals in the market or how to borrow money at the lowest interest rate. Those are all useful things to know, but the mental tools and essential principles needed to analyze and evaluate the paramount issues of the day are too often missing.

Moreover, even a cursory examination of textbooks used in high school economics courses reveals a dismal level of understanding or outright bias by the text authors themselves. Students are sometimes reading, for instance, that Americans are undertaxed, that government spending creates new wealth and that politicians are better long-term planners than private entrepreneurs. It is not uncommon for texts to portray free market competition and private property in a suspicious light while presenting government intervention with little or no critical scrutiny. It therefore may actually be a blessing rather than a curse that so few students are exposed to what passes these days in the schools as "economics."

Stripped of bias, the study of economics is immensely important. Indeed, without it we miss an understanding of much of what makes us the unique, thinking creatures we are. Economics is the study of human action in a world of limited resources and unlimited wants — a lively topic that cannot be reduced to lifeless graphs and mind-numbing equations that occupy the pretentious planner's time.

Economics teaches us that everything of value has a cost. It informs us that higher standards of living can come about only through greater production. It tells us that nations become wealthy not by printing money or spending it, but through capital accumulation and the creation of goods and services. It tells us that supply and demand are harmonized by the signals we call prices and that political attempts to manipulate them must produce harmful consequences.

Economics explains that good intentions are worse than worthless when they flout inexorable laws of human action. It reminds us to think of the long-term effects of what we do, not just the short-term or the flash-in-the-pan effects. It tells us a great deal about the critical role of incentives in shaping human behavior.

In short, economics is a blueprint for a free and sound economy, which is indispensable to satisfying human material needs and wants. When the subject is well understood, people learn that leaving other people alone is a far more likely path to well-being than shoving them around with political dictates.

When people have little or no economic understanding, they embrace the "quick fix" and support impractical "pie-in-the-sky" solutions to problems. They may think that whatever the government gives must really be "free," and that all it has to do to foster prosperity is to command it.

Economically illiterate people are easy prey for currency cranks who argue that manufacturing more money will make us wealthier. They may even think that trade is a bad thing — that if we shut the borders to the flow of goods our living standards will rise. They will be unable to identify economic snake oil, and also untrained to detect its harmful consequences.

Arguably, America's great economic problems have their roots in widespread ignorance of economic principles. When the noted economist John Maynard Keynes was asked in the late 1930s if we should be concerned about rising debt and printing press money, he reportedly responded with this flippant remark: "In the long run, we're all dead." Today, as the late Henry Hazlitt countered, is the tomorrow that yesterday's bad economists like Keynes told us we could safely — but wrongly — ignore.

Americans are being asked every day to form judgments, make choices or cast votes for programs and proposals that are largely economic in nature. It would behoove us to start talking about how we provide the missing tools we need to make those and other such decisions, so that we don't dig ourselves deeper in the muck of poor thinking and bad public policy.

So, you say, the answer is to mandate the teaching of economics! If the schools aren't teaching the subject, well then, let's *make* them do it! Oh, there's that tempting but utterly counterproductive "quick fix" again — a symptom, in fact, of the very illness I am describing.

Passing laws to require the teaching of economics, as some states have already done, is precisely *not* the answer. That only politicizes the subject and guarantees that too many people who don't understand it or don't want to teach it are instructing bored youngsters who couldn't care less. The vast majority of public school teachers are decent citizens of good will and great talent, but as government employees they labor in an environment naturally hostile to the critiques of government action that sound economics inevitably produces.

The idea of government-mandated economics teaching strikes me as likely to be no more effective than government-mandated teaching of anything else. Aren't we in the midst of a national education crisis as it is, with test scores and other measures of student aptitude plummeting to disgraceful levels? Is there any reason to believe that government can teach us economics any better than it teaches us mathematics?

The remedy for America's economics knowledge deficit is really the same remedy for our general knowledge deficit: a combination of demonopolizing the education system and diligent self-instruction.

If economics is as important as I've suggested, then a market-driven, choice-focused, performance-based and fully accountable education system would surely do a better job of teaching it than a government monopoly that gets subsidized whether it teaches for the real world or not. Make education a product of the marketplace instead of politics, and much more than just economics will be taught (and taught well).

Formal schooling, though, even in a thoroughly privatized environment, can be only part of the economics teaching equation. What we learn on our own, especially if we hope to inspire and persuade others, may be just as important. Looking back on my own economics training, I note that most of it was under the auspices of private groups like the Foundation for Economic Education and by way of publications such as The Freeman.

In any event, the relative absence of economics from America's classrooms is a problem that requires our attention. Many private efforts to solve it deserve our support. But no one should be fooled into thinking that putting government in charge will resolve it.

September 1994

Making the Case for Liberty Stick

Rolling back an intrusive, overweening government is no simple task. A remarkably tenacious creature, it spares no expense as it struggles to retain its grip on society. It is greatly aided in that fight by many of those who rely on transfer payments for all or part of their livelihood. Meanwhile, the liberty of all the people hangs in the balance.

Pointing fingers, naming names and unmasking duplicitous politicians are tactics that can never by themselves win the battle for liberty. Indeed, such tactics can be counterproductive when they lull people into thinking that changing faces in government is enough to change results. Ideas must change, and if they do, the faces will take care of themselves.

For some, focusing on ideas seems to be an unbearably long-term strategy. They yearn for the magic button that, when pressed, will make things better. They think everything depends on who gets into office in the next election. They want to win elections now, so they put their money and time into yard signs and bumper stickers instead of books, articles, seminars and other educational tools.

These impatient friends fail to understand that politicians rarely operate outside a box framed by public opinion, which, translated, means the demands and expectations of those politicians' particular constituencies.* One wealthy patron of hundreds of candidates over the years recently expressed this frustration to me: "I wish I could do something so that once the people I support get elected I won't have to keep calling them to find out why they cast so many bad votes and make so many wrong decisions." I told him that the one most effective thing he could do is to invest in ideas. "Give someone a book," I told him, "not a bumper sticker."

Making the case for liberty stick, so that it isn't simply some short-term rhetorical exercise, is a multifaceted task. It draws support from a range of intellectual disciplines — economics, political science, sociology and history, to name a few. It requires a nurturing of many personal virtues — self-reliance, enterprise, respect for others and their property, moral inspiration and optimism about what free people can accomplish. It encourages a patient, long-term perspective over the instant gratification of short-term

---

* This "box" of popular opinion was described and analyzed by Joseph P. Overton (to whom this anthology is dedicated), and the concept subsequently came to be known as the "Overton Window of Political Possibilities." Overton emphasized the need to shift the window of the "politically acceptable" towards liberty, an idea that became an integral part of the strategies for a freer society among market-oriented think tanks.

obsessions. To this list I add one more ingredient that is worthy of our increased attention — *demystifying government.*

Too many battles are lost to statists because of a misplaced and hard-to-shake faith in government itself. For all its endless failures, now more widely perceived than at any time in decades, government is still regarded as real and tangible while free-market alternatives are often thought of as nebulous and imaginary.

For example, take Social Security. Most Americans now acknowledge its inherent flaws and impending debacle. Suggest ending Social Security and making retirement security a purely personal and market-based responsibility and many of those same people wince in fear. "Who would take care of Grandma?" they ask. Of course, they want you to answer with a list of names and addresses; anything less will leave them in grudging acceptance of the status quo.

Far too many Americans think that if government provides education, it may do so ineffectively but at least some basic level of schooling will exist. Likewise, they think that if government gets into the low-income housing business, the result may be scandal-ridden but at least the poor will be housed.

It constantly amazes me that defenders of the free market are expected to offer certainty and perfection while government has only to make promises and express good intentions. Many times, for instance, I've heard people say, "A free market in education is a bad idea because some child somewhere might fall through the cracks," even though in today's government schools, *millions* of children are falling through the cracks every day.

Our task as friends of the free market is to reverse this state of affairs. We must portray the promises of government and politicized society for what they are — nebulous and imaginary. We must explain the benefits of free markets and civil society for precisely what they are — real and tangible. After all, isn't the evidence on these points overwhelming? Where do oppressed people flee when given the chance — to free countries or socialist countries? Where do they conquer more poverty by producing more goods that sustain life the longest and at the highest levels? In which environment do people attain the greatest satisfaction and self-fulfillment — an environment of dependency and sloth, or one of self-reliance and effort? Americans should be embarrassed even to ask such questions.

"The Myth of the Magical Bureaucracy," a booklet co-authored by four members of Congress, demystifies the federal government with a goldmine of facts and figures. For example, Americans have come to assume that since Washington became involved in education in the mid-1960s, education has been advanced; efforts to abolish the Department of Education and its 760 separate programs have been met with stiff resistance.

These are the facts: Educational performance in the United States has been in steady decline since the mid-1960s. Average SAT scores have dropped 35 points since 1972. Sixty-six percent of 17-year-olds do not read at a proficient level. U.S. students scored worse in math than all other large countries except Spain. Thirty percent of all college freshmen must take remedial classes.

For another example, consider the AmeriCorps program, which propagates the myth that magical bureaucrats can create a renewed volunteer spirit in America. The facts are these: AmeriCorps displaces true volunteerism by paying people with tax money to do good. Designed in 1993 to cost taxpayers only $16,000 per volunteer, three years later it costs between $25,797 and $31,017 per volunteer. Worse yet, only $14,000 of that money goes to the actual volunteer, while the remaining $11,000 to $17,000 goes to overhead and administration!

Making the case for liberty stick will take a lot more of this sort of compelling analysis, marketed in an articulate fashion. The emperor has no clothes; we have to encourage people to take their blinders off and see reality.

December 1996

A NECESSARY SPRING

Joe Overton: Character for a Free Society

A person's character is nothing more and nothing less than the sum of his choices. You can't choose your height or race or many other physical traits, but you fine-tune your character every time you distinguish right from wrong and act accordingly. Your character is further defined by how you choose to interact with others and the standards of speech and conduct you uphold.

Ravaged by conflict and corruption, the world is starving these days for people of high character. Indeed, as much as anything, it is on this issue that the fate of individual liberty has always depended. A free society flourishes when people seek to be models of honor, honesty and propriety. It descends into barbarism when they abandon what's right in favor of self-gratification at the expense of others, when lying, cheating or stealing are winked at instead of shunned. Those who favor the steady advance of liberty must assign top priority to raising the caliber of their own character and learning from those who already have it in spades.

So it is good news for liberty when anyone, anywhere, commits his life to the loftiest standards of personal and professional behavior. It's bad news when we lose such models, and it is with profound sadness that I share some bad news with my readers. The world's sum of good character suffered an incalculable subtraction with the untimely death on June 30, 2003, of a friend and colleague, Joseph P. Overton. Killed in a tragic plane crash at the age of 43, barely three months after making his vows to the woman of his dreams at a picture-perfect wedding, he will be remembered by many lovers of liberty around the world as a man who displayed the highest character in every way.

Since his college days, Joe believed that liberty and character were mutually dependent, and he felt an irresistible calling to work for the advancement of both. He reached the zenith of his contributions as senior vice president at the Mackinac Center for Public Policy in Michigan, whose staff he joined in January 1992. You cannot walk an inch in our 23,000-square-foot headquarters without seeing his imprint — from the output of our organization to the very building itself, whose construction he supervised in 1997.

Talk to any one of our many employees, and you'll hear the same: His mere presence in a room would raise everyone's standards of speech and conduct. As a consummate administrator, he taught us the importance of continuous organizational improvement. He was able to do that effectively not just because he knew the nuts and bolts of the subject, but because he practiced it in his personal life as well. I heard him say many times, "You cannot impart what you don't possess."

Joe Overton was the straightest straight shooter I've ever known. Not a speck of deception, guile, conceit or hidden agenda in him. He said what he meant and meant what he said, *always*. You never, ever had to wonder if he was telling you the truth. He kept his word as if it were an indispensable and inseparable physical appendage like an arm or a leg. I came to place total, unqualified trust in him. So did others who came to know him.

Never underestimate the importance of truth and trust to a free society. If we cannot deal with each other on those terms, we will resort to the ugliness of brute force and political power.

Though packed into a few amazingly productive years, Joe's contributions to the international freedom movement were legion. He was known as a leader in the effort to liberate parents and children from the grip of the government school monopoly, and he designed a unique tax credit plan to move things in that direction. He devised winning strategies to liberate workers from compulsory unionism. And he created what is becoming known as the "Overton Window of Political Possibilities" — a teaching tool that gets people to understand the importance of putting ideas ahead of political action.

Over and over again, people were attracted to his work because of his sterling character. Friends marveled at his consistency and self-discipline. They were impressed that he not only preached the virtues of civil society; he practiced them in his own life through endless volunteer efforts, quiet philanthropy and ceaseless counsel to those who needed good advice. All of this comes through loud and clear in the hundreds of tributes to him that poured in from all over the world in the two weeks after the accident that claimed his life. As a testimony to his far-flung influence, within days of the tragedy a Joseph P. Overton Leadership Center was announced in Nairobi, Kenya, for the purpose of training African youth in the principles of liberty and how best to advance them.

So much more could be said of this great man, but I close with an excerpt from a eulogy I delivered at his funeral:

> The world needs more men who do not have a price at which they can be bought; who do not borrow from integrity to pay for expediency; who have their priorities straight and in proper order; whose handshake is an ironclad contract; who are not afraid of taking risks to advance what is

right; and who are as honest in small matters as they are in large ones.

The world needs more men whose ambitions are big enough to include others; who know how to win with grace and lose with dignity; who do not believe that shrewdness and cunning and ruthlessness are the three keys to success; who still have friends they made 20 years ago; who put principle and consistency above politics or personal advancement; and who are not afraid to go against the grain of popular opinion.

The world needs more men who do not forsake what is right just to get consensus because it makes them look good; who know how important it is to lead by example, not by barking orders; who would not have you do something they would not do themselves; who work to turn even the most adverse circumstances into opportunities to learn and improve; and who love even those who have done some injustice or unfairness to them. The world, in other words, needs more true leaders. More to the point, the world needs more Joe Overtons.

October 2003

As Values Collapse, Government Grows

In 1995, students on the quiz team at Steinmetz High School in Chicago made national news when it was discovered that they had cheated to win a statewide academic contest. With the collaboration of their teacher, they had worked from a stolen copy of a test to look up and memorize the correct answers in advance. Perhaps worse than the initial deed is the attitude of the same students five years later, expressed in the New York Times by one of them this past May: "Apologize for what? I would do it again."

The collapse of ethical values in American society, of which the Steinmetz case is but one example, is frighteningly real, and it didn't start last month. Ten years ago, 65 percent of high schoolers in a Louis Harris poll said, "Yes, I would cheat to pass an important exam." Fifty-three percent said they would lie to protect a friend who has vandalized school property. When asked, "What do you take to be the most believable authority in matters of truth?" between 1 percent and 2 percent said science or the media. Between 3 percent and 4 percent said religion or parents. But most of the kids said "me." In another survey, 67 percent of high school seniors said they would inflate an expense account; 50 percent, pad an insurance claim; and 66 percent, lie to achieve a business objective.

"Moral Illiteracy" of American Students
Students answering 'yes' to the following questions:
In the past year, have you ...

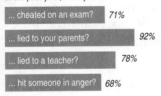

... cheated on an exam? 71%

... lied to your parents? 92%

... lied to a teacher? 78%

... hit someone in anger? 68%

Source: The Josephson Institute of Ethics.
"Report Card on the Ethics of American Youth." October 2000

These and other manifestations of a national ethical vacuum were cited in a remarkable speech in 1991 by noted ethicist Rushworth Kidder. He recounted a true story about a 10-year-old child who found a wallet full of money, credit cards and identification. The boy took the wallet into school and was unable to find either a teacher or an administrator who would tell him what the right thing to do with the wallet was. "I can't possibly impose my values on you," Kidder said the teachers and administrators seemed to be saying.

At the core of America's ethics crisis is the destructive notion that ethics are in the eye of the beholder, that there are no "absolutes" against which the actions and decisions of people should be judged. Ethics has been relegated to a values-neutral approach, where the teacher, in Kidder's words, "is not to get in the way of kids discovering their own ethical standards." Distinctions between right and wrong are being eroded. Indeed, it seems that many people think fewer and fewer things are really "wrong" when their "context" or the individual's motives are taken into account.

In the decade since the Harris poll and the Kidder speech, things have not improved. The nonpartisan Joseph & Edna Josephson Institute in Los Angeles reported that the "hole in the moral ozone" remains highly disturbing.

Ethical relativism, or "non-ethics," has suffused its poison throughout society — a major reason America seems to be losing its moral compass. But that isn't the only thing we're losing. The first casualty when the ethical core of society evaporates is freedom. Law (government) fills the void — directing by threat of force those aspects of life that formerly were governed by our ethical standards.

Ethical people don't require the threat of fines to keep them from tossing trash out of car windows or for embezzling funds from their employer, because ethical people don't do those things. Nor do ethical people abandon responsibility for the education of their children or the care of their parents and expect others to do the job. Ethical people don't cast off their problems onto others. They have both a healthy dose of self-esteem and a respect for the lives and property of others. The choice, in other words, is to govern yourself or be governed. The less you do of the former, the more you will get of the latter.

Ultimately, the standards by which we order our personal lives and our relationships with family, associates and others shape the heart of our society. When those standards are strong, people take care of themselves and those around them; they work for a living instead of voting for one. When those standards decay, we pay the price in broken families, crime, drug abuse, child neglect and greater reliance upon public welfare. If the rot gets deep enough, the price can be reckoned in terms of national bankruptcy and dictatorship.

Restoring our ethical foundations ought to be the top priority for all Americans. There's just too much at stake for us to do otherwise.

November 2000

The True Meaning of Patriotism

Patriotism these days is like Christmas — lots of people caught up in a festive atmosphere replete with lights and spectacles. We hear reminders about "the true meaning" of Christmas — and we may even mutter a few guilt-ridden words to that effect ourselves — but each of us spends more time and thought in parties, gift-giving and the other paraphernalia of a secularized holiday than we do deepening our devotion to the true meaning.

So it is with patriotism, especially on Memorial Day in May, Flag Day in June and Independence Day in July. Walk down Main Street America and ask one citizen after another what patriotism means and with few exceptions, you'll get a passel of the most self-righteous but superficial and often dead-wrong answers. America's Founders, the men and women who gave us reason to be patriotic in the first place, would think we've lost our way if they could see us now.

Since the infamous attacks of Sept. 11, 2001, Americans in near unanimity have been "feeling" patriotic. For most, that sadly suffices to make one a solid patriot. But if I'm right, it's time for Americans to take a refresher course.

Patriotism is *not* love of country, if by "country" you mean scenery — amber waves of grain, purple mountain majesties and the like. Almost every country has pretty collections of rocks, water and stuff that people grow and eat. If that's what patriotism is all about, then Americans have precious little for which we can claim any special or unique love. And surely, patriotism cannot mean giving one's life for a river or a mountain range.

Patriotism is not blind trust in anything our leaders tell us or do. That just replaces some lofty concepts with mindless goose-stepping.

Patriotism is not simply showing up to vote. You need to know a lot more about what motivates a voter before you judge his patriotism. He might be casting a ballot because he just wants something at someone else's expense. Maybe he doesn't much care where the politician he's hiring gets it. Remember Dr. Johnson's wisdom: "Patriotism is the last refuge of a scoundrel."

Waving the flag can be an outward sign of patriotism, but let's not cheapen the term by ever suggesting that it's anything more than a sign. And while it's always fitting to mourn those who lost their lives simply because they resided on American soil, that too does not define patriotism.

People in every country and in all times have expressed feelings of something we flippantly call "patriotism," but that just begs the question. What is this thing, anyway? Can it be so cheap and meaningless that a few gestures and feelings make you patriotic?

Not in my book.

I subscribe to a patriotism rooted in ideas that in turn gave birth to a country, and it's these ideas that I think of when I'm feeling patriotic. I'm a patriotic American because I revere the ideas that motivated the Founders and compelled them, in many instances, to put their lives, fortunes and sacred honor on the line.

What ideas? Read the Declaration of Independence again. Or, if you're like most Americans these days, read it for the very first time. It's all there. All men are created equal. They are endowed not by government but by their Creator with certain unalienable rights. Premier among those rights are life, liberty and the pursuit of happiness. Government must be limited to protecting the peace and preserving our liberties, and doing so through the consent of the governed. It's the right of a free people to rid themselves of a government that becomes destructive of those ends, as our Founders did in a supreme act of courage and defiance more than 200 years ago.

Call it freedom. Call it liberty. Call it whatever you want, but it's the bedrock on which this nation was founded and from which we stray at our peril. It's what has defined us as Americans. It's what almost everyone who has ever lived on this planet has yearned for. It makes life worth living, which means it's worth fighting and dying for.

I know that this concept of patriotism puts an American spin on the term. But I don't know how to be patriotic for Uganda or Paraguay. I hope the Ugandans and Paraguayans have lofty ideals they celebrate when they feel patriotic, but whether or not they do is a question you'll have to ask them. I can only tell you what patriotism means to me as an American.

I understand that America has often fallen short of the superlative ideas expressed in the Declaration. That hasn't diminished my reverence for them, nor has it dimmed my hope that future generations of Americans will be reinspired by them.

This brand of patriotism, in fact, gets me through the roughest and most cynical of times. My patriotism is never affected by any politician's failures, or any shortcoming of some government policy, or any slump in the economy or stock market. I never cease to get that "rush" that comes from watching

Old Glory flapping in the breeze, no matter how far today's generations have departed from the original meaning of those stars and stripes. No outcome of any election, no matter how adverse, makes me feel any less devoted to the ideals our Founders put to pen in 1776. Indeed, as life's experiences mount, the wisdom of what giants like Jefferson and Madison bestowed on us becomes ever more apparent to me. I get more fired up than ever to help others come to appreciate the same things.

During a recent visit to the land of my ancestors, Scotland, I came across a few very old words that gave me pause. Though they preceded our Declaration of Independence by 456 years and came from 3,000 miles away, I can hardly think of anything ever written here that more powerfully stirs in me the patriotism I've defined above. In 1320, in an effort to explain why they had spent the previous 30 years in bloody battle to expel the invading English, Scottish leaders ended their Declaration of Arbroath with this line: "It is not for honor or glory or wealth that we fight, but for freedom alone, which no good man gives up except with his life."

Freedom — understanding it, living it, teaching it and supporting those who are educating others about its principles. That, my fellow Americans, is what patriotism should mean to each of us today.

June 2003

Who Owes What to Whom?

For a society that has fed, clothed, housed, cared for, informed, entertained and otherwise enriched more people at higher levels than any in the history of the planet, there sure is a lot of groundless guilt in America.

Manifestations of that guilt abound. The example that peeves me the most is the one we often hear from well-meaning philanthropists who adorn their charitable giving with this little chestnut: "I want to give something back." It always sounds as though they're apologizing for having been successful.

Translated, that statement means something like this: "I've accumulated some wealth over the years. Never mind how I did it, I just feel guilty for having done it. There's something wrong with my having more than somebody else, but don't ask me to explain how or why because it's just a fuzzy, uneasy feeling on my part. Because I have something, I feel obligated to have less of it. It makes me feel good to give it away because doing so expunges me of the sin of having it in the first place. Now I'm a good guy, am I not?"

It was apparent to me how deeply ingrained this mindset has become when I visited the grave site of John D. Rockefeller at Lakeview Cemetery in Cleveland a few years ago. The wording on a nearby plaque commemorating the life of this remarkable entrepreneur implied that giving much of his fortune away was as worthy an achievement as building Standard Oil, the great international enterprise that produced the wealth in the first place. The history books most students learn from these days go a step further. They routinely criticize people like Rockefeller for the wealth they created and for the profit motive that played a part in their creating it, while lauding them for relieving themselves of the money.

More than once, philanthropists have bestowed contributions on my organization and explained they were "giving something back." They meant that by giving to us, they were paying some debt to society at large. It turns out that, with few exceptions, these philanthropists really had not done anything wrong. They made money in their lives, to be sure, but they didn't steal it. They took risks they didn't have to. They invested their own funds, or what they first borrowed and later paid back with interest. They created jobs, paid market wages to willing workers and thereby generated livelihoods for thousands of families. They invented things that didn't exist before, some of which saved lives and made us healthier. They manufactured products and provided services, for which they asked and received market prices. They had willing and eager customers who came back for more again and again. They had stockholders to whom they had to offer favorable returns. They also had competitors, and had to stay on top of things or lose out to them. They didn't use force to get where they got; they relied on free exchange and voluntary contract. They paid their bills and debts in full. And every year they donated some of their profits to lots of community charities no law required them to support. Not a one of them that I know ever did any jail time for anything.

So how is it that anybody can add all that up and still feel guilty? I suspect that if they are genuinely guilty of anything, it's allowing themselves to be intimidated by the losers and the envious of the world — the people who are in the redistribution business either because they don't know how to create anything or because they simply choose the easy way out. They just take what they want, or hire politicians to take it for them.

Or like a few in the clergy who think that wealth is not made but simply "collected," the redistributionists lay a guilt trip on people until they disgorge their lucre — notwithstanding the Tenth Commandment against coveting. Certainly, people of faith have an obligation to support their church, mosque or synagogue, but that's another matter and not at issue here.

A person who breaches a contract owes something, but it's to the specific party on the other side of the deal. Steal someone else's property and you owe it to the person you stole it from, not society, to give it back. Those obligations are real and they stem from a voluntary agreement in the first instance or from an immoral act of theft in the second. This business of "giving something back" simply because you earned it amounts to manufacturing mystical obligations where none exist in reality. It turns the whole concept of "debt" on its head. To give it "back" means it wasn't yours in the first place, but the creation of wealth through private initiative and voluntary exchange does not involve the expropriation of anyone's rightful property.

How can it possibly be otherwise? By what rational measure does a successful person in a free market, who has made good on all his debts and obligations in the traditional sense, owe something further to a nebulous entity called society?

If Entrepreneur X earns a billion dollars and Entrepreneur Y earns two billion, would it make sense to say that Y should "give back" twice as much as X? And if so, who should decide to whom he owes it? Clearly, the whole notion of "giving something back" just because you have it is built on intellectual quicksand.

Successful people who earn their wealth through free and peaceful exchange may choose to give some of it away, but they'd be no less moral and no less debt-free if they gave away nothing. It cheapens the powerful charitable impulse that all but a few people possess to suggest that charity is equivalent to debt service or that it should be motivated by any degree of guilt or self-flagellation.

A partial list of those who honestly do have an obligation to give something back would include bank robbers, shoplifters, scam artists, deadbeats and politicians who "bring home the bacon." They have good reason to feel guilt, because they're guilty.

But if you are an exemplar of the free and entrepreneurial society, one who has truly earned and husbanded what you have and have done nothing to injure the lives, property or rights of others, you are a different breed altogether. When you give, you should do so because of the personal satisfaction you derive from supporting worthy causes, not because you need to salve a guilty conscience.

February 2002

Is There a Statesman in the House?[*]

In the aftermath of Hurricane Katrina, all Americans lament the death and suffering along the Gulf Coast. We grieve for those who have lost loved ones and precious property. We shudder at the cost of recovery and what it will mean for deficit-ridden federal and local budgets. But the spectacle of recent days painfully spotlights yet another deficit the country must come to grips with — a shortage of statesmanship.

The pre-Katrina story is a swamp of political malfeasance. Failure to properly prepare for such a contingency, even when dire storm warnings were bearing down on the region, raises serious questions about well-paid public officials asleep at the switch.

In the storm's aftermath, the statesmanship dearth is even more apparent. Many public officials are occupied with finger-pointing and political posturing. And they are outbidding themselves with other people's money, either to cover for their earlier failures or to demonstrate their "compassion." Thank God for the private sector, which in spite of roadblocks erected by government officials, has yielded a gusher of genuine compassion — quickly, efficiently and without saddling future generations with so much as a dime of the expense.

Will we find in this generation those truly exceptional leaders needed to chart a responsible course through such difficulties? Politicians are ubiquitous, but where are the statesmen? And what's the difference?

Statesmen are a cut above politicians, who seek office for the thrill of it or for the power it brings. Some politicians are better than others but statesmen rise above mere politics, the meat grinder of principles. The clever politician knows how to deftly manipulate the levers of power for personal advantage, but the statesman's allegiance is to loftier objectives.

A statesman doesn't seek public office for personal gain or attention. Like President Washington, he takes time out from a life of accomplishment to serve the general welfare. He stands for a principled vision, not for what he thinks citizens will fall for. He is well-informed about the vicissitudes of human nature, the lessons of history, the role of ideas and the economics of the marketplace.

---

[*] This article was co-authored with Burton W. Folsom Jr., Ph.D., a professor of history at Hillsdale College in Hillsdale, Mich., and a senior fellow in economic education at the Mackinac Center for Public Policy.

He is a truth-seeker, which means he is more likely to do what's right than what may be politically popular at the moment. You know where he stands because he says what he means and means what he says. He elevates public discussion because he knows what he's talking about. He does not engage in class warfare, race-baiting or other divisive or partisan tactics that pull people apart. He does not cynically buy votes with the tax dollars he takes from others. He may even judge his success in office as much by how many laws he repealed as by how many he passed. He takes responsibility for his actions.

When it comes to managing public finances — an especially relevant subject in light of massive appropriations for Katrina disaster relief — a statesman doesn't view government at any level as a fountain of limitless largesse. He prioritizes. In an emergency, he exhibits the courage to cut less important expenses to make way for the more pressing ones.

Washington, in his farewell address, urged his countrymen to avoid "the accumulation of debt, ... not ungenerously throwing upon posterity the burden which we ourselves ought to bear." His generation acquired the Revolutionary War debt, and his generation retired it. More than a century later, another statesman, Calvin Coolidge, vetoed popular programs to hold spending in check in order to pay off the debt his generation accumulated in World War I. He vetoed a bonus to Army veterans; he even vetoed twice the first large-scale farm subsidy proposed in U.S. history; he shunned short-term popularity with farmers for long-term financial security for his country. Every year of his presidency showed a federal budget surplus.

After World War II, another huge crisis, statesmen emerged to echo Washington's plea to bear our generation's debt responsibly. President Dwight Eisenhower, in his farewell address, surprised some by deploring the spending in his lifelong field of military defense. "We — you and I, and our government — must avoid the impulse to live only for today, plundering, for our own ease and convenience, the precious resources of tomorrow," Ike warned.

Statesmen would not saddle our children with debt from Hurricane Katrina. Yet Congress and the White House will spend tens of billions of dollars for the Gulf Coast without lopping more than a pittance off even the most obvious pork. For most of American history, disaster relief was primarily a private matter and secondarily a state and local government one. It was not a federal responsibility at all. For example, Washington, D.C., did not rebuild San Francisco after the 1906 earthquake. That was a remarkably successful private affair, with minimal involvement even from state and local governments.

Is it too much to ask Archer Daniels Midland to forgo its ethanol subsidies in the face of the disaster in the South? Is there a statesman in the House who will rise in defense of suspending aid to the Rock and Roll Hall of Fame in Cleveland or the Country Music Hall of Fame in Nashville? Can Sen. Ted Stevens be persuaded that not even a bridge to nowhere in Alaska is more important than keeping our monstrous debt from ballooning as help is sent to New Orleans?

Alas, if performance to date is any indication, America's political class has become a sorry lot — addicted to profligate spending, incapable of making sensible choices, oblivious to the trillions of debt to which it blithely adds billions more at the drop of a levee.

Perhaps we should all take a moment to thank our great-grandchildren, mostly unborn. If we lack statesmen in this generation, we will have our disaster relief, our pork and our politics and they will pay for much of it.

September 2005

WHAT IS REAL COMPASSION?

In the last election campaign, we heard the word "compassion" at least a thousand times. Democrats have it, Republicans don't. Big government programs are evidence of compassion; cutting back government is a sign of coldhearted meanness. By their misuse of the term for partisan advantage, politicians have thoroughly muddied the real meaning of the word.

The fact is that much of what is labeled "compassionate" is just that, and it does a world of good; but much of what is labeled "compassionate" is nothing of the sort, and it does a world of harm. The former tends to be very personal in nature while the latter puts an involuntary burden on someone else.

As Marvin Olasky points out in "The Tragedy of American Compassion," the original definition of compassion as noted in The Oxford English Dictionary is "suffering together with another, participation in suffering." The emphasis, as the word itself shows — "com," which means with, and "passion," from the Latin term "pati," meaning to suffer — is on personal involvement with the needy, suffering with them, not just giving to them. Noah Webster, in the 1834 edition of his American Dictionary of the English Language, similarly defined compassion as "a suffering with another."

But the way most people use the term today is a corruption of the original. It has come to mean little more than, as Olasky puts it, "the feeling, or emotion, when a person is moved by the suffering or distress of another, and by the desire to relieve it." There is a world of difference between those two definitions: One demands personal action; the other, simply a "feeling" that usually is accompanied by a call for someone else — namely, government — to deal with the problem. One describes Mother Teresa or the Salvation Army, the other describes Massachusetts Sen. Edward Kennedy or the Washington welfare lobby.

The plain fact is that government compassion is not the same as personal and private compassion. When we expect the government to substitute for what we ourselves ought to do, we expect the impossible and we end up with the intolerable. We don't really solve problems, we just manage them expensively into perpetuity and create a bunch of new ones along the way.

From 1965, the beginning of the so-called War on Poverty, to 1994, total welfare spending in the United States was $5.4 trillion in constant 1993 dollars. In 1965, total government welfare spending was just over 1 percent of gross domestic product, but by 1993 it had risen to 5.1 percent of GDP annually — higher than the record set during the Great Depression.

The poverty rate today is almost exactly where it was in 1965, perhaps even slightly higher. Millions live lives of demoralizing dependency; families are rewarded for breaking up; and the number of children born out of wedlock is in the stratosphere — terrible facts brought about, in large part, by "compassionate" government programs.

A person's willingness to spend government funds on aid programs is not evidence that the person is himself compassionate. Professor William B. Irvine of Wright State University in Dayton, Ohio, explains, "It would be absurd to take a person's willingness to increase defense spending as evidence that the person is himself brave, or to take a person's willingness to spend government money on athletic programs as evidence that the person is himself physically fit." In the same way as it is possible for a "couch potato" to favor government funding of athletic teams, it is possible for a person who lacks compassion to favor various government aid programs; and conversely, it is possible for a compassionate person to oppose these programs.

It is a mistake to use a person's political beliefs as the litmus test of his compassion. Professor Irvine says that if you want to determine how compassionate an individual is, you are wasting your time if you ask for whom he voted; instead, you should ask what charitable contributions he has made and whether he has done any volunteer work lately. You might also inquire into how he responds to the needs of his relatives, friends and neighbors.

True compassion is a bulwark of strong families and communities, of liberty and self-reliance, while the false compassion of the second usage is fraught with great danger and dubious results. True compassion is people helping people out of a genuine sense of caring and brotherhood. It is not asking your legislator or congressman to do it for you. True compassion comes from your heart, not from the state or federal treasury. True compassion is a deeply personal thing, not a check from a distant bureaucracy.

The next time you hear the word "compassion," ask the person invoking it if he really knows what he's talking about.

January 1997

Growing Up Means Resisting the Statist Impulse

A few months ago, I walked into a restaurant in Naples, Fla., and said "A nonsmoking table for two, please." The greeter replied, "No problem. All restaurants in Florida are nonsmoking by law. Follow me."

For a brief moment as we walked to our table, I thought to myself: "Good. No chance of even a whiff of a cigarette. I like that!"

Then I felt shame. I had fallen victim to the statist impulse. For 40 years, I thought I was a passionate, uncompromising believer in the free society. Yet for a few seconds, I took pleasure in government trampling on the liberties of consenting adults in a private setting.

This incident troubled me enough to think about it a long while. I wanted to know why my first instinct was to abandon principles for a little convenience. And if a committed freedom-lover like me can be so easily tugged in the wrong direction, what does that say for ever getting nonbelievers to eschew similar or more egregious temptations?

At first, I thought about the harm that many doctors believe secondhand smoke can do. Perhaps it wasn't wrong for government to protect nonsmokers if what we have here is a case of one person imposing a harmful externality on an unwilling other. Then I quickly realized two things: no one compelled me to enter the place, and the restaurant belonged to neither the government nor me. The plain fact is that in a genuinely free society, a private owner who wants to allow some people in his establishment to smoke has as much right to permit it as you or I have to go elsewhere. It's not as though people aren't aware of the risks involved. Moreover, no one has a right to compel another citizen to provide him with a smoke-free restaurant.

Besides, I can think of a lot of risky behaviors in which many adults freely engage but which I would never call upon government to ban: sky diving and bungee jumping being just two of them. Statistics show that merely attending or teaching in certain inner city government schools is pretty risky too — and maybe more so than occasionally inhaling somebody's smoke.

The statist impulse is a preference for deploying the force of the state to achieve some benefit — real or imagined, for oneself or others — over voluntary alternatives such as persuasion, education or free choice. If people saw the options in such stark terms, or if they realized the slippery slope they're on when they endorse government intervention, support for resolving matters through force would likely diminish. The problem is, they frequently fail to equate intervention with force. But that is precisely what's involved, is it not? The state government in Florida did not request that restaurants forbid smoking; it *ordered* them to under threat of fines and imprisonment.

I tried this reasoning on some of my friends. Except for the diehard libertarians, here were some typical attitudes and how they were expressed:

Delusion: "It's not really 'force' if a majority of citizens support it."

Paternalism: "In this instance, force was a positive thing because it was for your own good."

Dependency: "If government won't do it, who will?"

Myopia: "You're making a mountain out of a molehill. How can banning smoking in restaurants possibly be a threat to liberty? If it is, it's so minor that it doesn't matter."

Impatience: "I don't want to wait until my favorite restaurant gets around to banning it on its own."

Power lust: "Restaurants that won't keep smoke out have to be told to do it."

Self-absorption: "I just don't care. I hate smoke and I don't want to chance smelling it even if a restaurant owner puts the smokers in their own section."

On a larger scale, every one of these arguments can be employed — indeed, they are invariably employed — to justify shackling a people with intolerable limitations on their liberties. If there's one thing we must learn from the history of regimes, it is that you give them an inch and sooner or later, by appealing to popular weaknesses, they will take a mile. The trick is getting people to understand that liberty is more often eaten away one small bite at a time than in one big gulp, and that it's wiser to resist liberty's erosion in small things than it is to concede and hope that bigger battles won't have to be fought later.

Delusion, paternalism, dependency, myopia, impatience, power lust and self-absorption: All are reasons people succumb to the statist impulse. As I pondered this, it occurred to me that they are also vestiges of infantile thinking. As children or adolescents, our understanding of how the world works is half-baked at best. We expect others to provide for us and don't much care how they get what they give us. And we want it now.

We consider ourselves "adults" when we learn there are boundaries beyond which our behavior should not tread; when we think of the long run and all people instead of just ourselves and the here and now; when we make every effort to be as independent as our physical and mental abilities allow; when we leave others alone unless they threaten us; and when we patiently satisfy our desires through peaceful means rather than with a club. We consider ourselves "adults" when we embrace personal responsibility; we revert to infantile behavior when we shun it.

Yet survey the landscape of American political debate these days and you find no end to the demands to utilize the force of the state to "do something." Tax the other guy because he has more than me. Give me a tariff so I can be relieved of my foreign competition. Subsidize my college education. Swipe that property so I can put a hotel on it. Fix this or that problem for me, and fix it pronto. Make my life easier by making somebody else pay. Tell that guy who owns a restaurant that he can't serve people who want to smoke.

I wonder if America has become a giant nursery, full of screaming babies who see the state as their loving nanny. It makes me want to say, "Grow up!"

Societies rise or fall depending on how civil its citizens are. The more they respect each other and associate freely, the safer and more prosperous they are. The more they rely on force — legal or not — the more pliant they are in the hands of demagogues and tyrants. So resisting the statist impulse is no trivial issue.

In my mind, resisting that impulse is nothing less than the adult thing to do.

October 2006

THE TRIUMPHANT FUTURE

How We'll Know When We've Won

"Are we winning?" That's a query I hear almost every time I speak to an audience about liberty and the battle of ideas. Everyone wants to know if we should be upbeat or distraught about the course of events, as if the verdict should determine whether or not we continue the fight. Too many friends of liberty rely on the prevailing wind to tell them whether, when and how to proceed — and even how to feel about it at any given moment.

Personally, I try to take a long-term, optimistic, even-tempered and self-directed approach that doesn't depend upon the rest of the world. Each of us ought to do all we can to advance the cause and then let the proverbial chips fall where they may, taking comfort in the fact that we did our best as individuals, regardless of the outcome. Moreover, I remain supremely confident that, as Foundation for Economic Education founder Leonard Read put it, "truth will out," and liberty will indeed triumph, *because it is right*. Pessimism is a self-fulfilling opiate anyway, so I never let it enter my mind.

But this begs an even more important question, one posed to me recently when I cited powerful intellectual trends as evidence that we are indeed winning. The question was, "How will we know when we've won?"

In the largest sense, "winning" means achieving a civil society in which people both preach and practice respect for life and property. It means we each mend our own ways and mind our own business. It means we rely upon voluntary association and individual compassion, not coercive arrangements and political redistribution. It means minimal government and maximum self-reliance. And when we get there, the battle of ideas will still not be over because people, being less than perfect, can always unlearn the truths they've learned.

In a narrower, more concrete sense, we'll know we've won when very specific changes — in thought and policy — have come about. I've compiled a few here in a list that is by no means complete. Consider it a beginning.

We'll know we've won ...

• *When "liberalism" once again is synonymous with liberty.*

In his "History of Economic Thought," Joseph Schumpeter noted that liberalism initially described the view of those who believed that "the best way of promoting economic development and general welfare is to remove fetters from the private enterprise economy and to leave it alone."

In today's American parlance, it means quite the opposite. Schumpeter regarded it as "a supreme, if unintended, compliment" that "the enemies of the system of private enterprise have thought it wise to appropriate its label."

Liberalism is too good a term to allow it to be the booty of statists. Let's retake it, and let those who fight to preserve the failed big-government status quo be known as the real "conservatives." When that happens, we'll have won much more than just the semantic high ground.

• *When "public service" is regarded as what one naturally does in the private sector.*

Government employment, even when the employee is running roughshod over the rights and property of others, wears the prestigious mantle of selfless service to humanity, a cut above what motivates people who *don't* work for the government. But in many cases, a government worker's genuine public service actually begins when he secures an honest living in the private sector — producing goods and providing services that improve the lives of others who patronize him because they choose to, not because they're forced to.

Conquering diseases, inventing labor-saving devices, feeding and clothing millions, and countless other private, often profit-motivated activities are no less indicative of service to the public than just about anything the government does. The next time someone tells you he's running for office or seeking a government job, ask him if this means he is planning to leave public service.

• *When an "entitlement" is a paycheck, not a welfare check.*

My hat's off to whoever started the bad habit of calling government handouts "entitlements." The term cleverly solidifies and perpetuates the very programs it labels — programs that take something of value from those who earned it and bestow it on those who didn't earn it and may even value it less.

A paycheck for work performed is a genuine entitlement. A claim against that paycheck by those who would rather vote for a living than work for one is neither genuine nor something to which one is entitled in a free society. Let's correct the thought patterns that allow the current misuse of the term to undergird the modern welfare state.

- *When citizens muster at least as much interest in a
  spending revolt as they often exhibit for a tax revolt.*

Almost everyone favors lower taxes, at least for himself, but that doesn't
necessarily mean everyone also favors less government spending.
Sometimes, the same people who advocate lower taxes are in line for
whatever they can slurp from the public trough.

It's not enough to ask your congressman not to take from you. You must
also demand that he not give you anything either, at least nothing that
isn't rightfully yours in the first place.

- *When government stops distributing its
  coercive powers to special interests.*

Government isn't the only outfit that employs legal and often unwarranted
force against people. Others do it, too, if government first grants them the
power to do so.

The best example is today's labor unions. With special privileges
given them by government, they force millions into their ranks or into
financially supporting causes to which they may object. For instance,
the U.S. Supreme Court affirmed in its 1988 Beck decision the right
of each and every worker not to be assessed a penny by his union for
political activities without his consent, but almost no one at any level of
government seems interested in enforcing that ruling.

We should work for the day when a citizen's Beck rights are widely
regarded to be as important as his Miranda rights.

- *When self-improvement is understood to be the
  indispensable first step to reforming the world.*

If every person set about to make himself a model citizen, he would
have a full-time, lifetime job on his hands. Many succumb, however, to
the temptation to meddle in the affairs of others — and even the best of
intentions often ends up yielding conflict and harm.

The steady progress of mankind derives from the progress of individual
men and women who, one at a time, decide to make the best of what
God gives them. Be a model, not a burden, and watch how quickly you
encourage others to be the same.

A pretty tall order, you say? Yes, it is, and there are plenty of other benchmarks I could have added to this list to make the order even taller. Few things that are worthwhile are attained or retained easily. Winning the battle for liberty is among the most animating contests I can imagine, in part because the benchmarks along the way are as right as is the ultimate objective.

October 1997

REVIVING A CIVIL SOCIETY

"Taxes," said Oliver Wendell Holmes Jr., "are what we pay for civilized society." But as my fellow columnist Mark Skousen explained in his monograph "Persuasion vs. Force," a much better case can be made that taxation is actually the price we pay for the *lack* of civilization. If people took better care of themselves, their families and those in need around them, government would shrink and society would be stronger as a result.

Skousen put it well when he stated in a recent interview, "[E]very time we pass another law or regulation, every time we raise taxes, every time we go to war, we are admitting failure of individuals to govern themselves. When we persuade citizens to do the right thing, we can claim victory. But when we force people to do the right thing, we have failed." The triumph of persuasion over force, people helping people because they want to and not because government tells them they must, is the sign of a civilized people and a civil society.

For all people interested in the advancement and enrichment of our culture, this is a crucial observation with far-reaching implications. Cultural progress should not be defined as taking more and more of what other people have earned and spending it on "good" things through a government bureaucracy. Genuine cultural progress occurs when individuals solve problems without resorting to politicians or the police and bureaucrats they employ.

When the French social commentator Alexis de Tocqueville visited a young, bustling America in the 1830s, he cited the vibrancy of civil society as one of this country's greatest assets. He was amazed that Americans were constantly forming "associations" to advance the arts, build libraries and hospitals, and meet social needs of every kind. If something good needed doing, it rarely occurred to our ancestors to expect politicians and bureaucrats, who were distant in both space and spirit, to do it for them. "Amongst the laws which rule human nature," wrote de Tocqueville in "Democracy in America," "there is none which seems to be more precise and clear than all others. If men are to remain civilized, or to become more so, the art of associating together must grow and improve."

It ought to be obvious today, with government at all levels consuming upwards of 40 percent of personal income, that many Americans don't think, act and vote the way their forebears did in de Tocqueville's day. So how can we restore and strengthen the attitudes and institutions that formed the foundation of American civil society?

Certainly, we can never do so by blindly embracing government programs that crowd out private initiatives or by impugning the motives of those who raise legitimate questions about those government programs. We cannot restore civil society if we have no confidence in ourselves and believe that government has a monopoly on compassion. We'll never get there if we tax away 40 percent of people's earnings and then, like children who never learned their arithmetic, complain that people can't afford to meet certain needs.

We can advance civil society only when people get serious about replacing government programs with private initiative, when discussion gets beyond such infantile reasoning as, "If you want to cut government subsidies for Meals on Wheels, you must be in favor of starving the elderly." Civil society will blossom when we understand that "hiring" the expensive middleman of government is not the best way to "do good," that it often breaks the connection between people in need and caring people who want to help. We'll make progress when the "government is the answer" cure is recognized for what it is — false charity, a cop-out, a simplistic nonanswer that doesn't get the job done well, even though it makes its advocates smug with self-righteous satisfaction.

Restoring civil society won't be easy. Bad habits and short-term thinking die hard. It is especially difficult to get the civil society message through the major news media's filter unscathed. A recent editorial in a major Michigan newspaper is a good case in point. In arguing against suggested cuts in the state's budget, the editorial equated the restoration of civil society with subjecting human life "to the largesse of the highest bidder in the marketplace." What a shame that so many newspapers will routinely lament the superficiality of political campaigns and then employ bumper-sticker slogans when it comes to serious proposals to remove the bane of Big Government from our lives.

That editorial did not feed, clothe or house a single needy person. It probably did very little to comfort the afflicted. It did not inspire a single act of voluntarism on behalf of a troubled family. It may, however, have lulled some readers into a deeper sleep of complacency. Government, after all, is taking care of things, and that, the editorial implied, is as it should be.

Meanwhile, more thoughtful writers are noticing encouraging trends in the country. A remarkable article in the Jan. 29, 1996, issue of U.S. News & World Report trumpeted the "revival of civic life." Among the examples it cited was that of Frankford, Pa. Frankford had become a highly taxed, depressed and government-dependent community desperate for answers. A spark of civil society was lit, and now people are solving problems themselves. "When a record 30 inches of snow was dumped on the city, ... Frankford didn't stand around moaning about the inefficiency of city workers. Residents rented snowplows and split the cost," the article noted.

Perhaps if de Tocqueville were to visit this little Pennsylvania town today, he would see a glimmer of America's greatness in the 1830s. He would be impressed with the spirit of the community and might even suggest that Americans everywhere should take note. The citizens, de Tocqueville might remark, are not sitting back, bemoaning their plight and editorializing about how the politicians should save them. "Once you get past the resentment of the government not doing it for you, you get it done yourself," one local resident put it.

We can learn a whole lot more from the Frankfords of the world than from those who think charity means spending someone else's money or just pontificating about social needs from behind a word processor. Restoring civil society requires that we "Just Say No" to shirking our personal responsibilities and expecting government to do for us what we can and should do on our own, within our personal lives, our families and our local communities. It requires us to think creatively about stimulating private initiative — and then just do it.

September 1996

Seven Principles of Sound Public Policy

When I first took the podium to deliver the speech reprinted below, I was addressing the Detroit Economic Club, a world-renowned forum for sharing ideas. But even with my natural optimism and the publicity associated with that prestigious venue, I never imagined the amount of attention "Seven Principles of Sound Public Policy" would receive in the days and years that followed.

By last count, I've given this address in about 100 different places, including probably 30 states and a couple dozen foreign countries. The text has been translated into at least 12 foreign languages, including Chinese, Korean, Spanish and Kiswahili. In a twist stranger than fiction, I was invited to deliver this speech at the People's University in Beijing. Readers familiar with my views or with the seven principles will no doubt be struck by the irony — and the victory — inherent in my espousing these principles in the heart of the world's largest communist state.

Why has interest in the seven principles exceeded all expectations? Looking back, I think it was due to a gamble I took when I first wrote and delivered this address. At the time, I began by telling the audience:

> I know that (the Detroit Economic Club) has heard many policy addresses by many leaders in government, business and academia — policy addresses that dealt in some detail with specific pressing issues of the day, from transportation to education to health care and countless other important topics. At the Mackinac Center for Public Policy, our specialty is researching and recommending detailed prescriptions for today's policy questions, and I thought about doing that very thing here today.

> But upon reflection, I decided instead to step back from the minutiae of any particular issue and offer you something a little different: a broad-brush approach that is applicable to every issue. I'd like us all to think about some very critical fundamentals, some bedrock concepts that derive from centuries of experience and economic knowledge. They are, in my view, eternal principles that should form the intellectual backdrop to what we do as policymakers inside and outside of government.

The reception the speech received that day and in the years since suggests that at bottom, people value a serious attempt to deal with issues that matter. They recognize that principles that can be expressed in simple words are not necessarily simplistic.

Moreover, they realize that approaching issues with an open mind does not mean approaching them with an empty one. After all, we've learned a few things over the centuries. It's not uninformed bias that prompts us to accept without debate the notion that the sun comes up in the east. It isn't blind ideology that tells us that a representative republic is superior to a dictatorship or monarchy. The general assumption that private property and free-market economies are superior to state ownership and central planning is no longer just an opinion; rather, it is now a settled truth for people who value reason, logic, facts, evidence, economics and experience.

* * *

The seven principles of sound public policy that I want to share with you are pillars of a free economy. We can differ on exactly how any one of them may apply to a given issue, but the principles themselves, I believe, are settled truths.

These principles are not original with me. I've simply collected them in one place and added a few illuminating stories. They are not the only pillars of a free economy or the only settled truths, but they do provide a solid foundation. In my view, if the cornerstone of every state and federal building were emblazoned with these principles — and more important, if every legislator understood and attempted to be faithful to them — we'd be a much stronger, much freer, more prosperous and far better-governed people.

ONE

Free people are not equal, and equal people are not free.

First, I should clarify the kind of "equality" to which I refer in this statement. I am not referring to equality before the law — the notion that you should be judged innocent or guilty of an offense based upon whether or not you did it, with your race, sex, wealth, creed, gender or religion having nothing to do with the outcome. That's an important foundation of Western civilization, and though we often fall short of it, I doubt that anyone here would quarrel with the concept.

No, the equality to which I refer is all about income and material wealth — what we earn and acquire in the marketplace of commerce, work and exchange. I'm speaking of economic equality. Let's take this first principle and break it into its two halves.

Free people are not equal. When people are free to be themselves, to be masters of their own destinies, to apply themselves in an effort to improve their well-being and that of their families, the result in the marketplace will not be an equality of outcomes. People will earn vastly different levels of income; they will accumulate vastly different levels of wealth. While some lament that fact and speak dolefully of "the gap between rich and poor," I think people being themselves in a free society is a wonderful thing. Each of us is a unique being, different in endless ways from any other single being living or dead. Why on earth should we expect our interactions in the marketplace to produce identical results?

We are different in terms of our talents. Some have more than others, or more valuable talents. Some don't discover their highest talents until late in life, or not at all. Tiger Woods is a talented golfer. Should it surprise anyone that he makes infinitely more money at golf than I ever could? Will Kellogg didn't discover his incredible entrepreneurial and marketing talent until age 46. Before he struck out on his own to start the Kellogg Company and sell breakfast cereal, he was making about $25 a week doing menial jobs for his older brother in a Battle Creek sanitarium.

We are different in terms of our industriousness, our willingness to work. Some work harder, longer and smarter than others. That makes for vast differences in how others value what we do and in how much they're willing to pay for it.

We are different also in terms of our savings. I would argue that if the president could somehow snap his fingers and equalize us all in terms of income and wealth tonight, we would be unequal again by this time tomorrow because some of us would save our money and some of us would spend it. These are three reasons, but by no means the only three reasons, why free people are simply not going to be equal economically.

Equal people are not free, the second half of my first principle, really gets down to brass tacks. Show me a people anywhere on the planet who are indeed equal economically, and I'll show you a very unfree people. Why?

The only way in which you could have even the remotest chance of equalizing income and wealth across society is to put a gun to everyone's head. You would literally have to employ force to make people equal. You would have to give orders, backed up by the guillotine, the hangman's noose, the bullet or the electric chair — orders that would go like this: Don't excel. Don't work harder or smarter than the next guy. Don't save more wisely than anyone else. Don't be there first with a new product. Don't provide a good or service that people might want more than anything your competitor is offering.

Believe me, you wouldn't want a society where these were the orders. Cambodia under the communist Khmer Rouge in the late 1970s came close to it, and the result was that upwards of 2 million out of 8 million people died in less than four years. Except for the elite at the top who wielded power, the people of that sad land who survived that period lived at something not much above the Stone Age.

What's the message of this first principle? Don't get hung up on differences in income when they result from people being themselves. If they result from artificial political barriers, then get rid of those barriers. But don't try to take unequal people and compress them into some homogenous heap. You'll never get there, and you'll wreak a lot of havoc trying.

Confiscatory tax rates, for example, don't make people any more equal; they just drive the industrious and the entrepreneurial to other places or into other endeavors while impoverishing the many who would otherwise benefit from their resourcefulness. Abraham Lincoln is reputed to have said, "You cannot pull a man up by dragging another man down."

Two
What belongs to you, you tend to take care of; what belongs to no one or everyone tends to fall into disrepair.

This principle essentially illuminates the magic of private property. It explains so much about the failure of socialized economies the world over.

In the old Soviet empire, governments proclaimed the superiority of central planning and state ownership. They wanted to abolish or at least minimize private property because they thought that private ownership was selfish and counterproductive. With the government in charge, they argued, resources would be utilized for the benefit of everybody.

What was once the farmer's food became "the people's food," and the people went hungry. What was once the entrepreneur's factory became "the people's factory," and the people made do with goods so shoddy there was no market for them beyond Soviet borders.

We now know that the old Soviet empire produced one economic basket case after another, and one ecological nightmare after another. That's the lesson of every experiment with socialism: While socialists are fond of explaining that you have to break some eggs to make an omelet, they never make any omelets. They only break eggs.

If you think you're so good at taking care of property, go live in someone else's house, or drive their car, for a month. I guarantee you neither their house nor their car will look the same as yours after the same period of time.

If you want to take the scarce resources of society and trash them, all you have to do is take them away from the people who created or earned them and hand them over to some central authority to manage. In one fell swoop, you can ruin everything. Sadly, governments at all levels are promulgating laws all the time that have the effect of eroding private property rights and socializing property through "salami" tactics — one slice at a time.

THREE
Sound policy requires that we consider long-run effects and all people, not simply short-run effects and a few people.

It may be true, as British economist John Maynard Keynes once declared, that "in the long run, we're all dead." But that shouldn't be a license to enact policies that make a few people feel good now at the cost of hurting many people tomorrow.

I can think of many such policies. When Lyndon Johnson cranked up the Great Society in the 1960s, the thought was that some people would benefit from a welfare check. We now know that over the long haul, the federal entitlement to welfare encouraged idleness, broke up families, produced intergenerational dependency and hopelessness, cost taxpayers a fortune and yielded harmful cultural pathologies that may take generations to undo. Likewise, policies of deficit spending and government growth — while enriching a few at the start — have eaten at the vitals of the nation's economy and moral fiber for decades.

This principle is actually a call to be thorough in our thinking. It says that we shouldn't be superficial in our judgments. If a thief goes from bank to bank, stealing all the cash he can get his hands on, and then spends it all at the local shopping mall, you wouldn't be thorough in your thinking if all you did was survey the store owners to conclude that this guy stimulated the economy.

We should remember that famed free-market economist Henry Hazlitt warned that today is the tomorrow that yesterday's poor policymakers told us we could ignore. If we want to be responsible adults, we can't behave like infants whose concern is overwhelmingly focused on self and on the here-and-now.

FOUR

If you encourage something, you get more of it; if you discourage something, you get less of it.

You and I as human beings are creatures of incentives and disincentives. We respond to incentives and disincentives. Our behavior is affected by them, sometimes very powerfully. Policymakers who forget this will do dumb things like jack up taxes on some activity and expect that people will do just as much of it as before, as if taxpayers are sheep lining up to be sheared.

Remember when George Bush (the first one) reneged under pressure on his 1988 "No new taxes!" pledge? We got big tax hikes in the summer of 1990. Among other things, Congress dramatically boosted taxes on boats, aircraft and jewelry in that package. Lawmakers thought that since rich people buy such things, we should "let 'em have it" with higher taxes. They expected $31 million in new revenue in the first year from the new taxes on those three things.

We now know that the higher levies brought in just $16 million. We shelled out $24 million in additional unemployment benefits because of the people thrown out of work in those industries by the higher taxes. Only in Washington, D.C., where too often lawmakers forget the importance of incentives, can you aim for 31, get only 16, spend 24 to get it and think that somehow you've done some good.

Want to break up families? Offer a bigger welfare check if the father splits. Want to reduce savings and investment? Double-tax 'em, and pile on a nice, high capital gains tax on top of it. Want to get less work? Impose such high tax penalties on it that people decide it's not worth the effort.

FIVE

Nobody spends somebody else's money as carefully as he spends his own.

Ever wonder about those stories of $600 hammers and $800 toilet seats that the government sometimes buys? You could walk the length and breadth of this land and not find a soul who would say he'd gladly spend his own money that way. And yet this waste often occurs in government and occasionally in other walks of life, too. Why? Because invariably, the spender is spending somebody else's money.

Economist Milton Friedman elaborated on this some time ago when he pointed out that there are only four ways to spend money. When you spend your own money on yourself, you make occasional mistakes, but they're few and far between. The connection between the one who is earning the money, the one who is spending it and the one who is reaping the final benefit is pretty strong, direct and immediate.

When you use your money to buy someone else a gift, you have some incentive to get your money's worth, but you might end up getting something the intended recipient really needs or values.

When you use somebody else's money to buy something for yourself, such as lunch on an expense account, you have some incentive to get the right thing but little reason to economize. Finally, when you spend other people's money to buy something for someone else, the connection between the earner, the spender and the recipient is the most remote — and the potential for mischief and waste is the greatest.

Think about it — somebody spending somebody else's money on yet somebody else. That's what government does all the time.

But this principle is not just a commentary about government. I recall a time, back in the 1990s, when the Mackinac Center took a close look at the Michigan Education Association's self-serving statement that it would oppose any competitive contracting of any school support service (like busing, food or custodial) by any school district anytime, anywhere. We discovered that at the MEA's own posh, sprawling East Lansing headquarters, the union did not have its own full-time, unionized workforce of janitors and food service workers. It was contracting out all of its cafeteria, custodial, security and mailing duties to private companies, and three out of four of them were nonunion!

So the MEA — the state's largest union of cooks, janitors, bus drivers and teachers — was doing one thing with its own money and calling for something very different with regard to the public's tax money. Nobody — repeat, *nobody* — spends someone else's money as carefully as he spends his own.

Six
Government has nothing to give anybody except what it first takes from somebody, and a government that's big enough to give you everything you want is big enough to take away everything you've got.

This is not some radical, ideological, anti-government statement. It's simply the way things are. It speaks volumes about the very nature of government.

You've got to keep your eye on even the best and smallest of governments because, as Jefferson warned, the natural tendency is for government to grow and liberty to retreat. You can't wind it up and walk away from it; it takes eternal vigilance to keep it in its place and keep our liberties secure.

The so-called "welfare state" is really not much more than robbing Peter to pay Paul, after laundering and squandering much of Peter's wealth through a costly bureaucracy. Somebody once said that the welfare state is so named because in it, the politicians get well and the rest of us pay the fare.

A free and independent people do not look to government for their sustenance. They see government not as a fountain of "free" goodies, but rather as a protector of their liberties, confined to certain minimal functions that revolve around keeping the peace, maximizing everyone's opportunities and otherwise leaving us alone. There is a deadly trade-off to reliance upon government, as civilizations at least as far back as ancient Rome have demonstrated.

When your congressman comes home and says, "Look what I brought for you!" you should demand that he tell you who's paying for it. If he's honest, he'll tell you that the only reason he was able to get you something was that he had to vote for the goodies that other congressmen wanted to take home — and you're paying for all that, too.

SEVEN

Liberty makes all the difference in the world.

Just in case the first six principles didn't make the point clearly enough, I've added this as my seventh and final one.

Liberty isn't just a luxury or a nice idea. It's much more than just a happy circumstance. It's what makes just about everything else happen. Without it, life is a bore at best. At worst, there is no life at all.

Public policy that dismisses liberty or doesn't preserve or strengthen it should be immediately suspect in the minds of a vigilant people. They should be asking, "What are we getting in return if we're being asked to give up some of our freedom?" Hopefully, it's not just some short-term handout. Ben Franklin advised us, "Those who would give up essential Liberty, to purchase a little temporary Safety, deserve neither Liberty nor Safety."

Too often today, policymakers give no thought whatsoever to the general state of liberty when they craft new policies. If it feels good or sounds good or gets them elected, they just do it. Anyone along the way who might raise liberty-based objections is ridiculed or ignored.

I yearn for the day when all Americans practice these seven principles. I think they are profoundly important. Our past devotion to them, in one form or another, explains how and why we succeeded so spectacularly as a nation. They are key to preserving that crucial element of life we call liberty, without which sound policy is a mirage.

October 2001

The Love of Power vs. the Power of Love

"We look forward to the time when the power of love will replace the love of power. Then will our world know the blessings of peace."

So declared British Prime Minister William Ewart Gladstone more than a century ago. His audience surely responded then the same way audiences would today — with universal, nodding approval. But the world, perhaps more so now than when Gladstone spoke, seethes with hypocrisy. Though we say we prefer love over power, the way we behave in the political corner of our lives testifies all too often to the contrary.

Gladstone was eminently qualified to say what he did, and he sincerely meant it. He was a devout man of faith and character, lauded widely for impeccable integrity in his more than six decades of public life. Four times prime minister, he still ranks as one of the few politicians who really did "grow" in office. He came to Parliament in the early 1830s as an ardent protectionist, opponent of reform and defender of the statist status quo. As he watched government operate from its highest levels, he evolved into a passionate defender of liberty. When he died in 1898, his admirers were proud of a Britain strengthened by his legacy of cutting taxes, bureaucracy and intrusive regulation. The Irish loved him because he fought hard to lighten London's heavy hand over Irish life. Biographer Philip Magnus believed that he "achieved unparalleled success in his policy of setting the individual free from a multitude of obsolete restrictions."

Gladstone knew that love and power are two very different things, often at odds with each other. Love is about affection and respect; power is about control. Someone who pursues power over others for his own personal advancement is rightly deserving of opprobrium. Gladstone's friend Lord Acton warned about how absolutely corrupting this can be. If love is a factor in such instances, it's more likely love of oneself than love of others.

When real love is the motivator, people deal with each other peacefully. We use force only in self-defense. We respect each other's rights and differences. Tolerance and cooperation govern our interactions.

Suppose we want to influence or change the behavior of another adult, or want to give him something we think he should have. This person has done us no harm and is in full command of his faculties. Love requires that we reason with him, entice him with an attractive offer or otherwise engage him on a totally voluntary basis. He is free to accept or reject our overtures. If we don't get our way, we don't hire somebody to use force against him. "Live and let live," as Americans used to say with more frequency than they do today.

When we initiate force (that is to say, when self-defense is not an issue), it's usually because we want something without having to ask the owner's permission for it. The 19th century American social commentator William Graham Sumner lamented the prevalence of the less noble motivators when he wrote, "All history is only one long story to this effect: Men have struggled for power over their fellow men in order that they might win the joys of earth at the expense of others, and might shift the burdens of life from their own shoulders upon those of others."

Adults necessarily exert great power over infants, whose very existence requires nearly constant attention, tempered by a strong and instinctive affection. By adolescence, the adult role is reduced to general supervision as the child makes more of his own choices and decisions. The child eventually becomes an adult empowered to live his life as he chooses and bear all the attendant risks and responsibilities.

In normal, healthy families during this nearly 20-year maturing process, a parent's power over a child recedes but his love only grows. Indeed, most people understand that the more you love a child, the more you will desire him to be independent, self-reliant and in charge of himself. It's not a sign of love to treat another adult as if he were still an infant under your control.

A mature, responsible adult neither seeks undue power over other adults nor wishes to see others subjected to anyone's controlling schemes and fantasies: This is the traditional meaning of liberty. It's the rationale for limiting the force of government in our lives. In a free society, the power of love governs our behavior instead of the love of power.

Consider what we do in the political corner of our lives these days and an unfortunate erosion of freedom becomes painfully evident. It's a commentary on the ascendancy of the love of power over the power of love. We have granted command of over 40 percent of our incomes to federal, state and local governments, compared to 6 percent or 7 percent a century ago. And more than a few Americans seem to think that 40 percent still isn't enough.

We don't trust the choices parents might make in a free educational marketplace, so we force those who prefer private options to pay twice — once in tuition for the alternatives they choose, and then again in taxes for a system they seek to escape.

Millions of Americans think government should impose an endless array of programs and expenses on their fellow citizens, from nationalized health insurance to child day care to subsidized art and recreation. We've already burdened our children and grandchildren, whom we claim to love, with trillions in national debt — all so that the leaders we elected and re-elected could spend more than we were willing to pay for.

We claim to love our fellow citizens while we hand government ever more power over their lives, hopes and pocketbooks. We've erected what Margaret Thatcher derisively termed the "nanny state" in which we as adults are pushed around, dictated to, hemmed in and smothered with good intentions as if we're still children.

If you think these trends can go on indefinitely, or if you think power is the answer to our problems, or if you think loving others means diminishing their liberties, you're part of the problem. If you want to be part of the solution, then consider adopting the following resolutions for this year and beyond:

- I resolve to keep my hands in my own pockets, to leave others alone unless they threaten me harm, to take responsibility for my own actions and decisions and to impose no burdens on others that stem from my own poor judgments.

- I resolve to strengthen my own character so I can be the model of integrity that friends, family and acquaintances will want to respect and emulate.

- If I have a "good idea," I resolve to elicit support for it through peaceful persuasion, not force. I will not ask politicians to foist it on others just because I might think it's good for them. I will work to free my fellow citizens by trusting them with more control over their own lives.

- I resolve to offer help to others who genuinely need it by involving myself directly or by supporting those who are providing assistance through charitable institutions. I will not complain about a problem and then insist that government fix it at twice the cost and at half the effectiveness.

- I resolve to learn more about the principles of love and liberty so that I can convincingly defend them against the encroachments of power. I resolve to make certain that how I behave and how I vote will be consistent with what I say. And I resolve to do whatever I can to replace the love of power with the power of love.

A tall order, to be sure. Let's get started.

May 2007

If you enjoyed this book, you may enjoy other publications of the Mackinac Center for Public Policy, the Michigan-based think tank directed by Lawrence W. Reed for more than 20 years. Just visit the Mackinac Center Web site at www.mackinac.org, or call the Center at 989-631-0900.

The Mackinac Center provides a free-market perspective on economic issues like state taxes, state spending, education, privatization, labor policy, property rights, state and federal regulation, and science, environment and technology policy. The Center promotes its views through timely commentaries, policy studies, periodicals, media interviews, events for targeted audiences and responses to requests from policymakers. The Center's objective is to educate Michigan residents on the value of entrepreneurship, private initiative and independence from government, taxation and distant bureaucracies. The Center recognizes, as our country's Founders did, that the preservation of liberty requires vigilance from each generation of Americans.

If you share this goal, you can make a generous contribution to the Mackinac Center for Public Policy in any amount today. The Center is a 501(c)(3) educational institute, and your donation is deductible on your federal income taxes.